# AMONG THE LEAVES
*Queer Male Poets on the Midwestern Experience*

# AMONG THE LEAVES
*Queer Male Poets on the Midwestern Experience*

## RAYMOND LUCZAK
### Editor

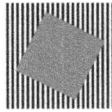

**SQUARES & REBELS**
Minneapolis, Minnesota

**ACKNOWLEDGMENTS**

The editor wishes to thank the following people for their help with this project in ways equally small and important: Ahimsa Timoteo Bodhrán, Bryan Borland, James Cihlar, David Cummer, Heid E. Erdrich, Deborah Keenan, Collin Kelley, Kate Lynn Hibbard, Kathryn Kysar, Kevin Luczak, John Medeiros, and Tom Steele.

The lines on the dedication page come from Walt Whitman's original sequence "Live Oak, with Moss." That version was unpublished during his lifetime.

*I dreamed in a dream of a city where all the men were like brothers,*
*O I saw them tenderly love each other—I often saw them, in numbers,*
*    walking hand in hand;*
*I dreamed that was the city of robust friends . . .*

FOR
DAVID CUMMER

"Wing Biddlebaum talked much with his hands. The slender expressive fingers, forever active, forever striving to conceal themselves in his pockets or behind his back, came forth and became the piston rods of his machinery of expression . . . The hands alarmed their owner. He wanted to keep them hidden away and looked with amazement at the quiet inexpressive hands of other men who worked beside him in the fields, or passed, driving sleepy teams on country roads."

— Sherwood Anderson, "Hands" (*Winesburg, Ohio*)

## The Slender Expressive Fingers, Forever Active

*by Raymond Luczak*

Certain poems have a way of picking you, much like the way a puppy climbs out of a litter and romps about, stops, considers you for a moment, and waddles over to you.

This anthology is a collection of such poems.

What is the Midwest? Technically, it encompasses twelve states in the upper middle half of the United States.

More importantly, the heartland is a perpetual state of mind, a place more pervasive than the literality of a land before them. There's something so indelible about having spent your formative years in a place where the land and its dramatic seasons leave their footprints all over your soul. We are forever bound to the land and its moods, which demand a great deal from us, so much that societal pressure pushes us into ill-fitting marriages, and sometimes more than enough to wonder why anyone should live in the Midwest. Such stories have been told over and over again, but in this anthology we get fresh glimpses in Jack Fritscher's "Clark Station: Kalamazoo 1969" and Malcolm Stuhlmiller's "The Piano Teacher."

The land upon which we grow up often becomes a force of nature whenever we reflect on those formative years. Christopher Hennessy's poems reveal the complexities of religion and nature. Whittier Strong's "Minnesota/Indiana" acknowledges the Midwest's schizophrenic nature—welcoming and uninviting. Christopher Leland's "If I Lived in New York" evokes how much living in the Midwest can give us a different perspective.

The seasons are inseparable from the land, particularly winter. William Reichard's poems here explore the shifts between warmth and winter, and an understated elegiac feeling informs Jim Stewart's work. If a poet is a photographer, then each poem becomes a snapshot, a remembrance of a certain time that is no longer our own. Gregg Shapiro's "Winter Work" is a sharp-eyed look at what it means to endure such a brutal season, and Christopher Hennessy's "Dreaming Through the Fifth Day Without Power" suggests the power of dreaming during such wintry days.

# FOREWORD

The pressure to conform can be so great that one's thoughts can turn to suicide. At 15, I wanted to kill myself. I was the only one deaf student in my hearing Catholic school, and my male classmates constantly picked on me. And when they weren't busy picking on me, they made sure that I knew I wasn't one of them. I didn't know how to fight back; no one had given me the language, the illuminations I would later discover in the work of gay poets before my time. Had I read Michael Kiesow Moore's poem "The Visitor" then, it would have given me great strength during my high school years.

Even then, it's difficult to talk back. My mother has always said, "If you can't say something nice about someone, don't say anything." The fear of offending anyone—or the gumption to dare doing so—runs strong in poems like Ahimsa Timoteo Bodhrán's "Repatriation," Brent Goodman's "How'd You Like It if I Called You a Jew?" and Stephen S. Mills's "This Side Up." James Schwartz celebrates the joys and the agonies of being an ex-Amish gay man finding himself in dance clubs full of men with poems like "Disco Rumspringa" and "Bad Behavior." In contrast, the sharp and precise language of James Cihlar's "How to be Manifold" feels like a K.O. punch against the Midwestern austerity.

The vexing question of budding masculinity versus the growing self-awareness of attraction to other men is always a potent one. Misinformed people have often considered homosexuality as "feminine," therefore not equal to heterosexuality. Although Christopher Leland's "Toward Valhalla" and Scott Wiggerman's "Plays Like a Girl" cover the same territory of playing football, they do so in markedly different ways. When we read work by heterosexual male poets, we're never surprised to find them discussing hunting, fishing, and so on—the very things that our dads are supposed to enjoy as a matter of tradition. It is a measure of how much times have changed that we are reading openly bisexual and gay poets such as Walter Beck ("Hoosier Swinging Both Ways Blues"), John Medeiros ("Camaraderie at the Super Bowl, 2005"), and Timothy Murphy ("Old Dog") talk about heavy metal, team machismo, and hunting.

Above all, the powerful need to connect with our own kind, whether in sexual terms or not, is the very river that runs throughout the entire land of this anthology. Here is the *real* heartland.

So: what does it mean to live out here in the Midwest, and to have lived it? Sherwood Anderson was among the first to try to convey something of that experience in so many words with his book *Winesburg, Ohio.* That was the first of my growing awareness of the Midwest as a unique place with a mindset all its own. Then came John Mellencamp's album *Scarecrow* and its look at the small town lives he'd known in Indiana. Of course, there were other musicians who lamented and celebrated the Midwest in their songs before him, but in the Golden Age of MTV in the 1980s, Mellencamp happened to be the first to make me go, "Hm. That's not New York or Hollywood." By then I was a college student living in Washington, D.C.

Then I became aware of *RFD*, a photocopied and stapled journal for radical faeries as well as gay men who'd chosen to live the rural life. They weren't into nightclubbing and wearing the latest fashions. Gay lives weren't limited to gay ghettos in large cities. Such choices seem so obvious now, but back then they were a revelation.

But the impetus for this anthology came from that moment of lightning when I stood near the magazine racks in the back of Lambda Rising, a gay bookstore in D.C. There, in front of me, was a copy of *The James White Review*, which was then printed as a folded newspaper. I was agog at the notion of a gay literary journal operating out of Minneapolis! Not New York, not San Francisco, not Los Angeles, but *Minneapolis, Minnesota?!?* The men who ran *JWR* had to have understood the Midwest in ways that many of my friends at Gallaudet University didn't. I wanted so badly to be part of what I imagined to be an exclusive club. Yet no matter what I submitted to them, I was rejected, occasionally with an encouraging handwritten note. Looking back, I realize my poems weren't ready for prime time. I had to discover my own voice first.

Here, in this collection, are a multitude of poets who have indeed found their own voices. How I've loved hearing them sing on the page, and how honored like a proud papa I am to bring these new songs out to be heard for the first time in print.

Each poem in this book has been chosen for a reason.

May all these poems choose you too.

It's my hope that this book will move you to reflect on what it meant to be a Midwesterner, therefore an American, back then and now.

As long as homophobia colors our attempts to connect with others different from us, we will need poetry more than ever, if only to validate our need to belong in such unforgiving times, and to celebrate our need to love whomever moves us, much like a puppy waddling over to us and accepting us unconditionally, to a love greater than us all.

As long as we live in the heartland, so will you.

# MALCOLM STUHLMILLER

## The Piano Teacher

*Play something for me,*
he says,
snuffing out a cigarette
in the great amber ashtray
already overflowing,
stinking the whole world
with stale butts.

*Play something you love,*
he says.
His smoke-stained fingers
stoke another filterless Camel
and beautiful blue acrobats
turn and tumble
in a circus of sunlight
between us,
stealing air,
making music our oxygen.

*Let the music speak for you,*
he says longingly,
remembering the car crash
that for two years
hospitalized his career
and still detonates his brain
with continuous cannons.
His potent hands,
delicately fondling the keys,
cannot muscle away the toccata
embracing his head,
always *allegro fortissimo,*
always relentless.

*First practice living—*
*then practice piano.*
Over and over he says this

like a father
forgiving his son's mistakes,
as the smoky breath
marks a musical phrase,
while black and white keys
patiently wait
for his flesh and bones
finally to grow into mine.

# MALCOLM STUHLMILLER

## Married

Three years after I learned from *Time* and *Newsweek*
that the New York queens had revolted,

I met my first man. A mortician.

Don't make anything more of that.
He was generous and ardent,

let me go as slowly as I needed,
let me think I was smarter than I was,

less afraid of myself than was possible.
He understood my fear and he understood the closet.

He didn't let on that he understood
but encouraged me to get married, have kids,

nobody would suspect a thing, he said,
if I let my married rank show

and played with the guys on the side.
And never tell your parents, he said,

it would break their hearts.

But *he* never married and had no children
of his own,

except for the 19-year old I was,
mummified alive on the North Dakota prairie.

## Bed

### 1.

Some mornings are too insistent,
so I linger
in your warm imprint,
absorbing
your unused sleep
after you vanish before dawn.
Then startled,
I ask, "What time is it?"
    Meetings, luncheons,
    news from the world,
    the sun low and diffused
    over people already in their suits,
    arguments, deals,
    hirings, firings,
    weddings, trysts,
    divorces.
Will I be late again?
Why did I cheat my sleep with Leno?
Is there milk for breakfast?
What's for dinner?

### 2.

The cats take turns
under the covers and on top,
looking for you.
They ask constantly—
Where have you gone so early?
When will you return?
Who will take care of us if you don't?
Five mornings a week
they miss the comforter
that is you.

# MALCOLM STUHLMILLER

On weekends they sleep
on the mountains and in the gullies
of your body,
while you complicate
their velvet ropes.


   3.

It isn't bothering anyone
if I don't make the bed every day.
It just lays there, confused,
as if hooligans crept in
smelling dimly of sleep, hair, armpits—
messed it all up, then fled
with my briefcase,
the scene of their crime
still tangled with evidence,
the sheets
with their little bears and stripes
thoroughly upset,
spilling over pinnacles,
through troughs,
crying out for law,
looking for order.
Bed is the battery
where the current of sleep
is stored,
waiting to be plugged into,
working while we sleep,
draining while we charge.

## Tequila

Some people struggle
to achieve low standards.
I have a mandate.

I am permitted to hate work.
I am allowed to despise power tools.
I am authorized in all circumstances
to appear lethargic about
my appearance,
to accept that I will waste
my genius watching TV,
to concede, loudly, to being
passive-aggressive.

My ambivalence
is single-minded.

I have vigorously catalogued
my indifference.

At best, my most positive attribute
can be said to be raising disconcern
to a high art form.

There was just a swallow left,
*100% puro de agave,*
so I had to finish it.
Golden it was.
A touch smoky.
Just enough to mix with the sour,
dry, scratchy circumstances
to which I find myself

soberly tethered.

# SCOTT WIGGERMAN

## Plays Like a Girl

*inspired by Michael Binkley's sculpture* Catch

Back then we didn't defy
coaches or fathers, didn't challenge
the red-blooded, all-American way,
so I had no choice but to play ball:
baseball, assigned to right field,
just me and swarms of no-see-ums;
basketball, my main goal to
be a "shirt" and not a half-naked "skin";
football, which at least afforded the anonymity
of lines of defense and tight huddles.
In every case, I longed to be on the bench.

This sculpture—
two white forms, fluid, whimsical,
so close together that even I
could catch the oversized ball
that hovers between them—
is everything my father and I were not.
I still flounce like a seal in an empty field,
my arms flapping in the air,
but I'll never catch if you don't let go.

## It Was Never about *Romeo and Juliet*

Randy was a high school rarity,
a boy with everything, loved by everyone:
jocks with whom he swung bats,
brains with whom he shared chemistry,
even the greasers he tutored in geometry.

I loved him for other reasons:
golden skin with a Scandinavian glow,
eyes as blue as clear June skies,
a jaw chiseled by Michelangelo.
Mostly because he was nice to me.

So when he asked if I wanted to go
to the school play with him that night,
I swooned as if this were a Dream Date.
When he pulled into the driveway
looking like a Ken doll in his convertible,
I raced to the car and told him to step on it,
though I had just told my dad that I was only
stepping out to let Randy know I'd been grounded.

I fully expected my father to arrive,
make a scene, drag me home,
and banish me to my room for life—
he wasn't used to being defied.
But I knew I might never have another chance
to share an armrest with Randy's wheat-haired arms—
my dad's wrath a poison I was willing to take.

# SCOTT WIGGERMAN

## Hate Crime

A man invites a stranger home from a gay bar,
wanting only a touch of love, not its opposite:
sexual assault, threats of death, a massive scar.

The stranger slams a glass in his face, a crowbar
up his ass. "It's what you want, isn't it?"
A man inveighed by a stranger. Home with a gay bar

patron, a bald-headed guy who smoked a cigar,
drank Miller all night, while planning to commit
sexual assault with threats of death. A massive scar

bulges from his tense neck, "I'm following an order
from above. He wants me to do this, you fucking faggot!"
The man invokes the stranger, "My home!" The gay bar

seems years ago, desire like a schoolgirl's memoir.
"Please, take anything," he whispers from a pool of vomit.
Sexual assault, the threat of death, a massive scar—

none are enough for the Aryan with the handlebar
moustache, who continues to stomp, kick, and hit
the man, the invert, a stranger. This home like a gay bar

with its queer stench, he finally heads to his car
and gloats, not a note of concern for the affadavit:
*A man invites a stranger home from a gay bar.*
*Sexual assault. Threats of death. A massive scar.*

## Skin Trade

In those days I still bought porn,
on the sly—but so did you.
My magazines were hidden
in accordion folders
labeled *Works in Progress*
and *Needs Revision*.
Yours were stacked
in your bedroom closet,
delicious wedges of sin.
When you weren't home,
I had the double pleasure
of rummaging through your things
and languishing over theirs.

We parted like an accidental drowning.

But not before I took
scissors to the collection
like a small-town librarian
excising profanities from her books—
only I cut out cocks.
With the precision of a lapidary,
I cut, I cut, I cut:
long, fat, pink, and brown,
wrinkled, ruddy, squat, and erect,
stubby cigars and slim cigarettes;
smooth, hooded, curved, and hooked,
hairy, veiny, greased, and scary.

I pawed through the pile
of odd and exotic species,
sorting, arranging, pasting,
creating a collage of cocks
to mail to you—
none exactly like yours,
a bit of you in every one.

# SCOTT WIGGERMAN

## Moonstruck

Already at the edge
of the bed, I struggle for space,
your arms like constrictors,
your breath a steam engine
chugging against my neck.

Outside the window,
an iridescent iris
fills the lens of the night.
I lie still, transfixed,
my will to fight struck numb.

Suspended over the treeline
like a wayward prisoner,
the moon has never looked
so swollen or so lonely.

## Watching the Coots

*We are*: I know that is exactly what
is running through your heads right now. But I
refer to those cool birds, the *real* coots,
not me and not my partner. But that sigh . . .
That *is* me, though I hadn't intended
for you to hear. The back, the knee, can make
you moan involuntarily. Indeed,
you'll see. That rumble? It's just his stomach.
For fourteen years he's claimed it's talking back.
If this is middle age, we'll both be in
our hundreds, threatless coots beyond rebuke
for walking hand in hand. For now, two men
who watch the white-billed birds slightly apart,
our ruffled feathers waiting with one heart.

# JOHN MEDEIROS

## Song of Myself

*on googling my name online*

Who would have known
after all these years
I would come to master the art
of crafting jewelry?
That when my parents
emigrated from Europe
I would help make our new home
the international capital
of costume jewelry production?

And who would have dreamed
that I would build my empire
on a street I would later name
*John Medeiros Way,*
and provide polishing assistance
and stone setting services
to the precious metals industry by day,
while at night,
as the moon found her place in the sky
and all the real jewelers have closed their shops,
I would sneak away
like an elf in the dark
to create my own line of accessories?

*Real jewelry,* I'll tell them,
*crafted from non-precious stones.*

*Rhodium is harder than platinum,*
*and lasts twice as long,* I'll say.
*My cubic zirconium*
*(prong-set and never glued)*
*is tougher than sapphire,*
*and can scratch glass like natural diamonds.*

And who would have thought
after all these years

that a jeweler in New England
bearing my name
would come to master the fine art
of taking medication
to stay alive?

Each pill like tiny gemstones—
throat-coating in their subtlety—
some orange, some white,
others diamond-shaped and star-freckled
like the face of an evening sky in summer.
All of them resting in the palm of his hand like precious jewels
before glistening on his tongue for a moment
while he imagines the flavor
of soft caramel.

# JOHN MEDEIROS

## Camaraderie at the Super Bowl, 2005

*Damned Patriots*, sighs
the man standing at the urinal
next to mine, tired & flaccid
like the fan of a losing team.
His head bowed in a combination
of shame and curiosity
as one eye moves its way
from his to my penis.

He's talking, of course,
of football, & I'm too flattered
by his audience to tell him
that I'm from New England,
that even though the Patriots
are part of my blood & upbringing,
I never did support them.

Until now.
This night.
With this man standing beside me.

It is only by fate that we find ourselves
now in this dark-lit & tired Midwestern stall.
& it is only by fate that I stand after all
these years, proud & erect, satisfied—
for the first time in my life—
to be on the winning team.

# What Didn't Happen

The plan was simple:
I was to tether my horse
at the nearest post and arrive
at the south minneapolis
coffee shop clad in armor
and tales of knighthood
and you were to arrive
like an unannounced crier
and confess the secrets
of your world unknown
and I was to listen eagerly
with the eyes of a child
and remind you that
even in 2002 chivalry
is not dead and you were
to marvel at the wonders
of my world and remind me
once again why we met
and the evening was to roll
itself out like a carpet at our
feet and the sky was to
consume us like a forest
of spearmint and ivy
and I was to tell you
I was born with the moon
in taurus and you were
tell me your favorite color
is green and I was to pretend
to listen as I yielded to your
voice and you were to smile
and make everything alright.

# JOHN MEDEIROS

## Snapshots

are all he collects, hidden in a long box
like some secret corpse. All these pictures coping
& struggling with themselves. The plastic beige

radio that caught only two AM stations on its best
night. Its orange light aglow like a flashlight sandwiched
between bed sheets; its songs carrying him like a magic

carpet to the jungle where the lion slept. There are men
jumping off bridges in his head. & cold turbulent
waves that open their hungry arms before the swallow.

Little boys swimming with each other unclothed
with bodies smelling of chlorine & almost sulphur.
& God as distant as Boston smiling down on boys

with clean knickers on Easter. Maybe someday he'll have
snapshots of today. He'll look back & see himself sitting
curled in a corner like a prisoner in Walpole, rocking back

& forth eating nothing but chalk to survive. He'll see
a man with a city between his legs once gay & alive
like Beirut before the war, before the rapes and pillages,

when the ruins were sturdy & erect and people came
from all over just to see. He'll watch himself long & thin
as a thread being sucked through the eye of a needle

& left amorphous & useless in his own quilt. Perhaps
purple mountains in fields of snow. Clouds like stars
on canvas skies. & he, unidentifiable if not for his eyes.

JOHN MEDEIROS

## Endecha (Funeral Song)

evening falls a monarch
& its sky stretches out
its six-fingered hand
& its moon spills
over the peninsula
the way time spills
over people.
another ghost drowns
off the lisbon coast.

all the souls within us
mourn the baby once
nursed by the breast
of a mother who still sings
songs of secret ships
& black-tattered shawls.

they mourn the boy
cradle-ripped—
the motherland
now barren.  a life
without latitude,
without longitude.
& songs sung
as though it mattered
*a noite é uma lembrança*
*que não escurece nada.*
*evening is a memory*
*that obsures nothing*:

not the breast,
nipple-cracked
nor the sudden loss
of children
or a mother's tongue.

QUEER MALE POETS ON THE MIDWESTERN EXPERIENCE

21

# AHIMSA TIMOTEO BODHRÁN

## Unfolding

how to reach, out to you, after all these, years apart, i write,
begin again, the lesson, of being with, and without, you,
waiting perhaps, to receive, or write this, you are, with me here, now.

## Kanienke

a place between desire and metal, smithing here, silver,
the weaving of baskets before fire, birds beaks cawing,
knowing our hunger, woven round, raon-raon seeking
red, finest of string, deepening into purple, inner white,
row upon row of beads, we gather here, paddle down to
water, coast the rest of the way in. here, the quiet of water,
us, a drifting boat, reaching toward shore.

# AHIMSA TIMOTEO BODHRÁN

## waterssong

Dipping inside the boat, as I push-pull water to, away, from me, toward shore, the channel changes, current, boat pushed right-left, up-down, forward and back. The boat is moved forward. You move forward. You are moving in something moving. More than air, earth, you feel in water the motion, know its and your liquidity, how things are not solid. You are more aware of the elements, on, in water, than on land. This orb hurtling through space, spinning, thousands and thousands of miles an hour, yet, everything seems still. You are not still in water, water still moving in, (all) around you. You cross the other side as much as the other side crosses you. You arrive and are the arrival. The land arrives, greets, as do the waters, part— there are different waters, waters in the waters. You know this now. There are waters in you—singing in your body.

The water laps gently against the shore.
This is how I want you to love me.

## Plateau

perhaps I will glide across the water to meet you.

the way our bodies join in creases, new geometries of
skin, angles adjacent, ancient as these hills, I find you on
the flats, tidal pools, after a day of travel, we come here to
rest: the plateau of each other, the lover's body.

# AHIMSA TIMOTEO BODHRÁN

## Repatriation

In the museum of our people, I take you by the hand, through the exhibits. It means something to kiss you here. By the exhibit on Native skateboarding and (land)surfing, I take your tongue into my mouth, and you, mine.

Interesting to think we are protected. Our art and bodies, for once, protected. People need to go through security to get to us.

Perhaps this is where we are most safe—behind glass, security guards.

People can't say shit—or there'll be consequences.

*You're gonna say something to two queer Native boyz in a Native museum, really?*

Who knew this is where our kiss-ins should be?

But less protest, and more affirmation.

We come home.

At places the general public can't enter with weapons.

Past the electric wands and electric gates, where you have to pay admission to see us.

Perhaps they will bring offering. Centuries in waiting.

Grand Entry.

Perhaps this is where queer powwows can occur. Where urban Indianz can go. Where we can make out. Have our 49er songs. Where we can imagine 1491.

# AHIMSA TIMOTEO BODHRÁN

We seal the deal with a kiss.

Amongst other works of art.

I take you here before I make love to you.

There is a pattern, processional. A protocol for mating.

I will take you here; then we will eat.

Then we will eat again.

You so good against my tongue.

You, the one treasure I stole from the museum.

Repatriated.

# BRENT GOODMAN

## Situational Comedies

*Stop barking!* my father barks
at the collies. Each dinner
another family's family floated
above his shoulder, sitcoms
competing against his gaze.
The noodle casserole still
too hot to touch. My reflection
pooling in a soup spoon. Only
the TV spoke from the living room,
making itself comfortable, touching
the furniture with a dim flickering hand.
The long blue couch where Mom
and us children sometimes sat.
Father's sunken reclining chair.

## Choosing Your Family

So what if your father taught you how to present
arms: the rifle was plastic. The best lesson
was caring less—sports, relatives, credit cards . . .

*Your only father,* your only mother pleads.

Showering boys invented gym class. Get real,
coming out is easy. Choosing your family
is the gift wanting no children teaches you.

# BRENT GOODMAN

## My God Only Wears Tidy Whities

my god only wears tidy whities
my god will return password-protected
my god carves bodies from sea salt and gentle fur
my god never said that "in person"
my god burns to detonate your sons
my god snores through baptisms
my god tides our lungs
my god only remembers one pose
my god hates fags
my god's hands cannot stop opening
my god lifts change from luck fountains
my god's fingers reflect funnel clouds and flies
my god prefers too many names to mention
my god walks among us as an animal
my god's mouth is wet and warm velvet
my god only wants us to want less

## How'd You Like It If I Called You A Jew?

It was the Jesus Christ Lizard's fault. Or my mom's
for watching the same *Nova* episode on PBS the night before,
but when my 3rd grade teacher suddenly slammed the TV
OFF, ripped the lightswitch UP, and spun around toward
ME, who moments prior delighted in the realization
I knew the TRUE name of the Basilisk Lizard BEFORE
the British documentary narrator revealed its miraculous
offense. On the screen, the snake-startled Basilisk
jumps off a branch onto the surface of a muddy pond
and bolts across the water RUNNING UPRIGHT while windmilling
two twiggy arms. In the darkened classroom I whispered
to some kid I don't recall ever having thought a friend
*Hey—that's the jesus christ lizard!*—words which also possessed
the mystical power to suddenly SHUT DOWN movie time
in Mr. *Welcome Back Kotter* hairdo's science class,
and before that little lizard could reach safe haven
the screen goes dark with an open-palmed WHACK
and the lights come blinding on, our teacher's chest
caved in slight horror. *Do you know how offensive that is?*
he asked all of us, my eyes as stung as everyone,
*How'd YOU like it if I called you a JEW?* his face
an open garbage can, then brittle, then calming.
I don't know how long his stare draped over us
or when the science lesson finally fell back into darkness.
I don't know which ME he was talking to, but I suspect
the one with a name as Jewish as his nose.
And when teacher hit PLAY and the narrator continued
*. . . this curious survivor who walks on water to escape danger
is commonly known as the Jesus Christ Lizard,*
it was as if on CUE. Like the Bible, this story has a hero
but we cannot find him. I know a 78-year-old Zen rabbi
whose last attachment is the Holocaust. But I'm
most attached to the part of the story I can't remember
because it's the closest I've ever come to silence.
I never imagined we could walk across water.
Truth is, that lizard taught me a lot about Jesus.

# BRENT GOODMAN

## Most the Time

Outside the Chicago Amtrak
waiting for the Van Galder
the man opening his palm to you
wears a teardrop tattoo
beneath his tired right eye.
Who do I become in any crowd,
besides the eyes of every window?
He wants to go somewhere
but has no money to get there.
I watch another woman offer
the "L" pass from her pocket
and the man's reluctant gratitude
roll her eyes. I trust I did too,
though I'm just a guy waiting
for a bus, schlepping
my suitcase wheels up
concrete curbs. I don't
want to guess when I should
fear another man's hand.
When in doubt or dream
I imagine every coincidence
of the scene must mean
something—the taxi driver's
open mouth, sun-dazzled
skyscrapers, the stranger
who sits down next to you
on the bus for three hours
north into Wisconsin through
a February snowstorm. A UW-Madison
Thai exchange student first time
feeling freezing on his way to study
microbiology in a "Christian dorm."
His knee against mine, see,
and at the end of the journey
I gave this man my wool gloves,
how he rubbed his bare hands

together as we talked, thin coat
far too soon for the season, and
whether downtown or alone or
in love, we're all just lights
in someone else's story, some
kind of lasting first impression,
right, to each other, or at least we
mean to be, most the time?

# TIMOTHY MURPHY

## Winter Camp: The Eagle Trail

Sleep in a cabin. I'm supposed to lead
for I'm the Eagle, just sixteen years old.
Minus forty Centigrade is cold,
the same as Fahrenheit. How shall I speed
my twelve-year-old charges up the trail?
Forty-nine of fifty falter and fail.

We were in Blackfoot Cabin, now long gone,
lucky we didn't die of white pine smoke.
Dreaming of it I wake up with a choke,
hoping, dear God, my nap will end with dawn.
Tomorrow, map and compass, axe and knife,
passages in an adolescent's life.

The great thing about Scouting is we give
authority to teenagers like me.
Teach every Tenderfoot to fell a tree,
give them twelve laws by which a boy can live,
grow up beside the wick of a gas lamp,
then send his sons north to Wilderness Camp.

## Mens sana in corpore sano

*on a line by Alan Sullivan*

### I. South Junior High

Twelve years old: an idiot phy ed teacher
made me wrestle a boy who far outweighed me,
who crushed two of my small cervical discs.
How to describe him? a sadistic creature.
    Well, there are certain risks
    in teaching physical fitness.
Today a trial lawyer would call a witness.
I ask, Was it that wrestling match that made me?


### II. Yale

First day of college at Payne Whitney gym:
    the step-up test on benches
    murderously wrenches
my back, but I complete the half-mile swim.

A doctor drops a plumb bob down my spine.
    "Incipient kyphosis
    and even worse lordosis,
but son, stand straight and someday you'll be fine."

Boys who are weak or fat must take phy ed,
    and though I feel abused,
    I pass, and I'm excused
to go to classes where they test your head.

# TIMOTHY MURPHY

## Epinikion Ode

### I.

It was on road cuts in the mountain West
I learned to read the rocks, the depositions,
igneous intrusions, the treasure chest
laid bare for us by contractors' incisions,
the dynamiting of a mountain's breast,
and the long scope of my Creator's visions.
The boy who taught me? God laid him to rest.

### II.

I cease to be a man of the Midwest.
It's fourteen years since last I sank a plough
in Svea-Beardon loam.  My heart turns now
west, to the rivers where the magpies nest.
Alan, I tried so hard to make a go
of dryland farming, couldn't make it work,
not that there was ever a task I'd shirk,
but luck wasn't with me. Where mountains grow
in man's imagination we sought relief—
on snow-covered massifs above the plains
thirsting so greedily for mountain rains,
the unforgiving fields that gave us grief—
the Wind River, Beartooth, the Bighorn peaks,
anything but this flatland where I farmed
and failed, as you grew ever more alarmed.
We drank too little from Wyoming's creeks.

### III.

Iguanas fall, half frozen, from the trees—
casuarinas—and the manatees
school by the outflows of the power plants

as Florida's mailmen pull on long pants.
Here it is lovely, seventeen above;
Feeney and I are flushing pheasants, love.

Fargo, of course, is buried deep in snow.
An age that you surpassed three years ago—
sixty—awaits me two weeks from today,
my waist still slim, my head still red, not gray,
my teeth rotten as timbers on a ship
the Spaniards left to settle in its slip:

my first birthday in thirty-seven years
without a partner to allay my fears
of growing old alone, of growing weak
as gravity defeats my frail physique,
of having no friend to replace the friend
who went so prematurely to his end.

I am forever, love, your tipsy rover:
*old sailors never die, they just keel over.*

# TIMOTHY MURPHY

## Way Gay

### I. Forty-Six Years Out of Sync

He's six feet two, and he is just sixteen.
    No, not a chance.
    I look askance
at one I'd jump, back when my waist was lean.

Were he to lay my red head on his shoulder
    what could I do?
    Propose we crew?
Better he be my solid, lofty soldier.

### II. Platonic Love

Endless affection,
undying attention,
immortal mention
and no erection.

### III. We Males

This little thing swinging above my balls?
It drives us, and its siren song, it calls.
We built our cities with our earthen walls,
and all male dreams end at Niagara Falls.

## Old Dog

Feeney, when you are gone, I'll just let go.
We've had enough of hunting in the snow.
I thank you for your two thousand birds
and thank you for my hundred thousand words.
We are collaborators on poetry.
A verse was lurking under every tree.

# JAMES CIHLAR

## Horoscope Revisited

Over the Wabasha Street Bridge,
an assortment of four or five clouds
comment on the sky.
The burled surface of the Mississippi
churns like a combustion engine.
Houses in Dayton's Bluff and Cherokee Heights
compete to tell their stories,
lives consigned either to heaven or to hell.
The city is laid out on the skyline
like a nude in an oil painting.
*You will alternate between two kinds of mindfulness.*
*One minute you're tuned into the people around you and the work at hand,*
*the next, you are focused on experiencing your inner world.*
Collect wherever you have been.
The brain is a garden, the ears factories.
Memory should not be passive.
Trees put up exclamations,
staple the hills to the moment.

## The Eighth Wonder of the World

I step on the natives to get to you.
I bite their heads off and spit them out.

Everyone knows I love you
But you. Take me to Manhattan.

One island is the same as another.
Put on your silk décolleté.

It's no different than a loincloth.
I'll writhe in chains for the upper crust

If it makes you happy.
You are my favorite toy.

# JAMES CIHLAR

## Bill's Room

*for Viola Reichard, Janesville, Minnesota*

The tenth of ten,
the room in the half-story
is referred to as his
but contains all.
Lining the drooping shelves,
artifacts of memory.
Boy gets car.
Is school hell?
Sweet sixteen.
Blood red wine.
The other.
Tips for teens.
Children grown,
children lost,
children moved away.
Above the living room,
the memory room.
Always close,
always safe.

## How to Be Manifold

First put the I in *team*.
Then press your start button.

Remember, the voice is not meant
to be used all the time.
You'll go blind.

In the past, the past was something
to be put behind us,
so as to get to the future
sooner.

The mind is not big enough
to hold a fortune.

Although we know
a fortune is forever,
and is unfinished,
we can only spend a little
at a time.

I'm going to blow out
the fourth wall
and open up your story.
In would I go.

Malevolent multitasker,
who wouldn't be drawn
to the raw wound
in the room?

You will never write a poem
as mean as me.

# JAMES CIHLAR

## Lying Down with Cats

Must let go of time.
Present and sound.

Hesitation, delicacy,
flash of pique.

Yes, curiosity.
Ecstatic tableaux.

Arced, coiled spines.
Extended arm grasping,

at last,
abandon.

## The Feline Wife

Curled in the crescent of the moon
fading into the window's milky light,
her body brings tides
into this Victorian house

on Cathedral Hill. Her glamorous face,
her ears a chapeaux worn in rakish tilt,
she is a lady putting on gloves,
a forties movie-star in black-and-white.

Or in sleep, her lax figure
is the natural stride of a champion racehorse
crossing the finish line,
then an awkward foal with limbs crossed,

or even the miracle of a hummingbird at rest.
Collectors describe a cookie jar
with a body and lid from two separate runs
a "marriage," even in Minnesota.

I with my papers and books,
she with her instinct
to lay a wounded mouse at my feet,
we make room in the house for each other.

# JAMES SCHWARTZ

## Disco Rumspringa

From sequestered settlements of Amish land,
My sequined *rumspringa* is at hand.
Away in the night I make my flight
To a world unknown lit by street light.

To Kalamazoo bars with the cabaret crowd,
Whiskey doubles and disco loud.
Miles from home and room to think.
A stranger's arms. Another drink.

From the plain people of the land,
Banning, damning, man and man.
To no bishop will I ever vow,
The stage is mine. I take my bow.

---

*The word "rumspringa" is a Pennsylvania Dutch word for the "running around" period in an Amish youth's life.*

## Stratford-upon-Avon Sonnet

Through darkest night he leads me to day.
Shedding his pillow for my head to lay.
To feast as beasts through hard techno beats' spray.
My salvation in man, I kneel to pray.
The cologne of his ale spinning my head.
Grunted lust of his thrust winning my hand.
The Stratford-upon-Avon bust by bed.
Sees spring drenched sonnets received like a man.
In the heat of the sheets and wet and sweat.
Hard Bard's work birthed in the here and now.
Even after limbs part, our lips have met.
After poems are penned the Muse shows me how:
The length of his desire and my rhyme.
Tireless strength that will burn the length of time.

# JAMES SCHWARTZ

## One Moon

Before I'm drunk and before I digress.
The hour grows late, no reason for leaving.
The air growing thick with throat and breath.
In state of undress, foggier breathing.
Only one moon for so many poets.
Do I dare ask for more? You shut the door.
Stealing my senses and taking my coat.
Making up miles and days away we bore.
Moonlight white the night, moonlight white the room.
Man on man silhouettes and sodomy.
Poetry conceived as fruit in a womb.
My moonlit ghost you are a god to me.
Taking me down with a kiss, nothing more.
Casting off clothing and closing the door.

## Morning in Michigan

His stubbled jaw in the dawn.
His sleepy, knowing smirk.

Empty bottles, echoes of laughter.
Pinnacle and piercing positions.

The sounds of humming vending machines and maids.
Drift down dim hallways.

Outside semis lumber onto I-80/90.
Factory workers and farmers breakfast.

Alone, driving home.
Drive-through coffee, and miles to go.

# JAMES SCHWARTZ

## Bad Behavior

I left the Order, never to return.
Everything to lose, bridges to burn.
Parties to partake, late night Jack.
Open roads, no turning back.

I left religion, no need of savior.
For disco lights and bad behavior.
A lonely warrior on my own.
Clubs close, no going home.

I left my family, fresh from the farm
For sin and gin and metro charm.
A stranger's touch and his voice.
Call to me, I've made my choice.

## Liberation

Man and man banned in damnation.
His kiss tasting of liberation.
In prayer position I fall blessed.
In sacred silence we undress.

Poems formed at first light.
Assumed positions, a finished night.
Abated appetites, sated heat.
Robotic rhythms refrain, repeat.

# STEPHEN S. MILLS

## To My Best Friend from High School Upon the Birth of His First Child

You are 800 miles away or maybe more—
I was never very good at math or directions,
which I'm sure you remember. Tonight,
you are likely walking the hallway of a house
I've never seen (never will) with a tiny creature
in your arms: pink, soft with a little poof
of brown hair like yours. You are a father
now, a teacher, a husband, someone
who will one day be called "a pillar
of the community." You are the Midwest
dream. The one that kept me up at night
all those years ago driving around cornfields
with you beside me. You planning your future,
me my escape. You are living my greatest
nightmare, though it fits you well like an old
suit jacket of your father's that one day simply
becomes you. We don't talk much anymore.
See, you spent your 20s laying the groundwork
for a comfortable life, a responsible life,
and I've spent mine living my lost rebellion
years. I drink too much. I stay up too late.
I spend most of my money on underwear
and books. I have more sex than I'm sure you
want to hear about, and not all of it is with
my boyfriend. But tonight, down here
in the heat of Florida, I'm awake and thinking
of the little boy in your arms, wondering
if he will ever hear the stories of a geeky red-
haired boy with freckles and his dorky best friend—
his father. Will you use our friendship
as a learning tool or a cautionary tale?
An unlikely pairing? Tonight, my hallway
is empty, quiet mostly, with only the snores
of another man at the end, behind a closed door.

## This Side Up

*for Mansoor*

In 7th grade I taught myself the five pillars of Islam:
        believe in only one God and that Muhammad
is his messenger, pray five times a day, give to the poor,
        fast the month of Ramadan,
and once in your life make pilgrimage to Mecca,
        and if you can't send your hair and fingernail clippings.
That city must be full of half-moon crescents,
        locks of graying hair—a city of human emissions.

It was the year I wanted to know what God looked like
        from the other side of the world, not the silent God
of my Quaker upbringing, but a God to fear,
        who gave rules, challenges, a God you died for.
Islam was dangerous or so I read in books with veiled women
        on the cover, or saw in Sally Field's face
as she vowed *not without my daughter*. I believed in her plight,
        in her view of the Islamic world,

one most Americans cared little about, until that Tuesday
        in September, my freshman year of college,
when the janitor, cleaning the dorm restroom, told me
        the world was ending. This just two weeks in,
two weeks of knowing my roommate, a Muslim from Pakistan,
        a nice guy who from time to time pulled out a rug,
asked which way was east, and knelt in prayer.
        His hands flat against the worn dorm carpet,

which had seen its fair share of naked flesh, crushed food,
        even vomit, but little prayer.
As the weeks went on, fear rose around us like the colors
        on the terror alert system the government
would later implement. Friends of my parents whispered:
        *if that was my son's roommate I'd have him removed immediately.*
As if he was making bombs in the bathroom sink,
        piling them in his backpack, and traipsing across

# STEPHEN S. MILLS

the campus green to blow up the old chapel,
    which served as the college theatre
of our small private school in Southern Indiana,
    the only place you can see three bends in a river,
it's a *Trivial Pursuit* question. Once he told me it was hard
    to be a Muslim in America with all the temptations,
and I don't know if he meant the girls who paraded the halls
    in tank-tops and short-shorts, which barely covered

their asses, or if he meant my temptations: the boys
    in their gym shorts, bare-assed in the showers,
or perhaps a more spiritual temptation, one that questioned
    everything, as he questioned me on all things
"American." Asking what exactly cheddar was, if I had friends
    like Joey from *Friends*, and if I knew the words
to "Jingle Bells" and would I please sing them for him.
    I never did. Once he attended *a Christmas*

that was *magical and beautiful*, and I thought how much
    he'd love my parents' house at Christmas,
their three themed trees, my father's Santa collection,
    and the lights he strung every year,
the day after Thanksgiving. Our house glowing
    for a month and a half. But I never invited
my roommate home to see our lights or eat our food
    or to meet my grandparents who might've said

something offensive. My world saw his world as dark—
    dark veils, dark deeds, dark skin, which I got peeks
of as he struggled to change beneath towels,
    always modest. And he saw America like me—
naked, presumably unashamed as bright city lights,
    which burn the eyes like spending hours
in front of the TV in complete darkness, then emerging
    in daylight, unaware, stumbling for something,

which I often did those two years I lived with him.
    Ashamed, I hid gay magazines in my top drawer,

him asleep in his golden comforter, his glasses
      on the nightstand. Later I'd creep into the bunk
above, thinking of 7th grade, of the five pillars, Sally's daughter,
      and of the world outside our room, the one
with crumbling towers and Middle-Eastern men body-searched
      in airports, attacked on streets, the bright lights buzzing

overhead. I never told him I was gay. One day I simply said:
      *I'm moving out*, and he looked surprised, sad even,
as if he wanted to stop me. Two years later at graduation,
      both in cap and gown, we shook hands, congratulated
each other, and laughed at some memory of us together,
      which may or may not have happened,
but I never said what I wanted to say, that he gave me
      that glimpse of God I had once longed for,

and that I was sorry about the night I didn't stop him
      from cooking his microwave popcorn
with the plastic wrapper still on. That instead I stepped
      into the hallway and waited for it to be over,
expecting a mess, my microwave in pieces, him crouched
      on the floor needing my help, but there he was
unharmed, the bag miraculously popped, the melted wrapper
      stuck to the side, both of us not saying a word.

# STEPHEN S. MILLS

## Frank O'Hara Wrote a Poem Called "Olive Garden"

and I wish it was about the chain restaurant,
but that would mean O'Hara didn't die in 1966,
that the beach taxi on Fire Island just missed
him. His friends calling out in the dark, relieved
to hear Frank drunkenly calling back, *Oh!*
*kangaroos, sequins, chocolate sodas!* It would also
mean he lived until 1982, when Olive Garden
opened its doors. The same year I was born
in Indiana to parents who never read Frank
O'Hara, or smoked cigarettes, or drank alcohol,
or sucked boys off in movie theatres. They
were good Christian parents who took my sisters
and me to Olive Garden on special occasions:
birthdays, anniversaries, good grades. I wonder
what O'Hara's poem would've been about
if he had stumbled into an Olive Garden
in the mid-80s. What would've captured
his imagination? The bustling waitresses delivering
*Tours of Italy*? Or how about the big-haired mothers,
the corduroy pants, or me in a brightly striped
polo that matched my father's? Or maybe the ass
of the busboy bending over clearing wine glasses,
cursing at the families smiling for pictures,
attempting to blend into the Midwest landscape
of strip malls, high school basketball games,
and church swim parties? A world I never fit into,
but that was before I met a boy to love, read
O'Hara, and moved to Florida where I still
sometimes go to Olive Garden to look at the walls
with their painted-on windows exposing
romanticized Italian landscapes. It's there I find
Frank running naked through the countryside,
his backside glowing in the setting sun.

## Trying to Convince My Aunt to Vote Democrat, 2008

Maybe I should start by telling her how I booed a robotic
George W. Bush at the Hall of Presidents in the Magic
Kingdom at Walt Disney World. Of course I'd leave out

the fact that I was drunk, had snuck rum in a Nalgene bottle
in the main gates. But I'd be sure to mention how another
man joined my booing, how he validated my attempt to cause

social change. It's not entirely her fault that she buys into
the conservative mumbo jumbo. She went to a Bible college,
has had a hard life, and it seems the harder the life the more

likely you are to believe in God and war. And I think of being
young, watching *Chitty Chitty Bang Bang* in her living room
in Florida, where I now live in "sin" with another man,

where she no longer lives. She's in Indiana where billboards
announce: *One Nation Under Me* signed God and half-formed
fetuses populate posters stuck along roadsides. Yes, she's

in Indiana where she calls to tell me my rights don't matter,
that there are bigger issues than me and my "community"—
and all I can do is boo from 800 miles away.

# GEORGE KLAWITTER

## Mr. Tony as Nazi

In Boy Scout camp
he used to line us up
under the hot Michigan sun
and tell us how rotten we were.

He loved to punish (more jumping jacks,
less time for beads and crafts)
and watched us from the shade
of his iron-green jungle hat.

One day down in the shower room
he stood naked, shaving at the mirror,
with his enormous cock
dripping deep inside the sink.

We tried, "Hello, Mr. Tony."
But he just sneered at us.
Thank god for all the cypress trees,
the tamarack and sassafras.

Away from him on nature walks
we could become ourselves and laugh
before they brought us back to Mr. Tony
for the evening meal, campfire, and harangue.

## Boy in the Family

Burning inside I entered the human race
a moral cripple. The doctor knew and beat
my wretched pride until the tears convinced
him I had learned my shame. The nurses knew
and tried to wash the slime off my face,

but nothing took. I hobbled into heat,
a brat for love or lust. My uncles winced,
their hearts unreadable. My bony aunts grew
chickens in their smiles and marked the pace
I moved into their realm. They left a seat

for me among their bric-à-brac, and since
I couldn't thrive with men, I joined the crew
of women, kitchen gossip, a little mace
among their stew, silent tongue and feet
unnoticed, so I guessed. In their minced

and breaking lives I thrived. Together we slew
the philistines of men demanding space
and power. How we laughed our laughter neat
though crushed beneath men's sweaty flesh,
convinced the uncles would eventually come too.

# GEORGE KLAWITTER

## Toward Valhalla

I go back in time to join the team.
The musty smell of the locker room
hits me as I slip into the dark
I never knew, the heavy stench

of adolescence pulled by window fans
out into Peoria's unrepentant sun,
cool in the space I can only guess
was rife with the chatty camaraderie

of boys I sat beside in Algebra and Latin
but never had the guts to talk to,
glassed as they were in their strange fervor,
patois, and uncontrollable urges,

their talk of girls and weekend escapades,
rattlesnakes and pepper stew,
whores and beer and rock-'n-roll—
things I could only scare into my mind.

Instead I lazed into the school band
where chrome and clarinet were clean,
polished, meant for higher things, heaven,
above the football lair I never entered.

In the aerie I learned Sousa, Offenbach,
the thrill of conquering arpeggios Mozart
made a thousand years before, the baton
our simple sign of discipline and order.

On Friday nights we'd gather in the stands
where, flashed in blue and gold and feathers,
we'd celebrate the great athletic bods
who smashed themselves on the field below.

But now in dreams I'm one of them.
I don my jock and plastic codpiece,
lace my shoulder pads and place my helmet
on my Achilles head, my feet in Hector's shoes.

We start to chant our vulgar taunts
against the enemy we plan to crush.
We're pumped on sweet testosterone,
ready for the crash of leather, cleats, and bone.

But mostly we are one, lost in one organic
will to dominate, to shine before the crowd
that cheers us into tense heroics
as the gods who'll lead them into Valhalla.

# GEORGE KLAWITTER

## Midwest Men

When music saves a hidden soul,
the boy becomes a man.
Then all the hurts of yesterday
dissolve as best they can.

The taunting jeers of schoolyards
evaporate to air.
Surrounded by his brothers he
relaxes in their care.

With parents gone and family cold,
the darkness of the night
resolves itself to gentleness
as music renders light.

His choristers are seraphim
who help him preen his wings.
Each evening is a melody
whenever this man sings.

The broken soul surrounding him
is molded into joy.
The tenors and the baritones
help form a man from boy.

The chords ascend as anthems rise
above the clouds into the skies
where waiting arms extend above
the unity of men in love.

## The Glassblower

With fingers delicate as spider legs
he hands the rod into the waiting flame
and watches as the glass transforms into
a joy of color dancing underneath

his eyes. It resonates as he begs
his breath gently down the tube the same
as if in Eden he'd coax Adam through
a flesh and bone silicone sheath.

I take my treasure home but do not wash
it since his touches on the vase remain
sweet tinctures swimming in the winter light:

he's on the shelf radiating gouache,
pastel, acrylic, oil, and sand to tame
my soul trilling from that wild night.

# CHRISTOPHER LELAND

## Anagnorisis

Tulsa, in the Sooner State, is far from seas
as any place can be. Perhaps that's why
my father (reared in Baltimore)
presented me a book, he said, he cherished
as a boy: *The Tattooed Man.*

What was I? Eight or nine? A little runty,
somewhat sissy, destined for right field.
A bit too bookish; hence, why not a tome
that spoke of high adventure on the sea?

Todd, I think, the youth's name was—this a book
from when there first came boys,  then youths, then men.
He had stowed away, or was he Shanghaied? Or
talked his way onto that leaky freighter?

It had a lurid cover—vivid reds and
blues and yellows. At one edge, arms crossed
upon his chest, The Tattooed Man himself
stood burly, broad of shoulder, stubble-jawed,
his arms and shoulders sinuous with swirls
and clouds and dragons. Todd said that
inky dreams bloomed like a pelt upon
his back, his chest, his legs . . . Where else?

No doubt, my father never stopped to think
how that blond sailor might roll over his
young boy in swoony waves, relentless as
the sea itself. We'd both identify
with Todd, but my bed-thoughts turned toward
what happened late at night below the decks.

I couldn't know—a callow Oklahoma boy.
I had no word for lust. But all those
years ago, I felt some strange, electric
knowledge shudder through me.

## Dakota

Desperately, frantically,
there in a gas station men's room
out there in Dakota. You both
had known standing, the pumps in your hands,
what the both of you wanted and needed and
there in that heartland, it had been
a long time, a long time
and O how you noted
his eyes, yes, his eyes
how they jingled you, tingled you,
fell on you gropingly, hopingly,
O, how you felt them, and knew.

His stink was so wondrous,
so acid and thorough, and you
wanted him, wanted him;
he wanted you. The both of you
tasting each other. So fine, and
you knew that the farm, yes, the farm,
it was calling him, calling him,
she and the children, and
he, full of wanting—a
good man, a good man,
and so this brief loving—
this loving, a gift.

.

# CHRISTOPHER LELAND

## If I'd Stayed in New York

If I'd stayed in New York, I'd be famous now.
You'd've read my books. Yeah, you'd know my name.
You'd've seen my face in a magazine as
I made quite the splash on the cultural scene.

If I'd stayed in New York, I'd've had a kid
not exactly on purpose, just to say I did.
I'd've palled with Tama and Brett and Jay,
with Morgan and Gary. I'd've been their gay

connection to the boys of the Violet Quill.
I'd've straddled worlds. I'd've had my fill
of coke and kudos, bourbon and renown
from the stews of the baths to the clubs uptown.

If I'd stayed in New York, I'd've cruised the piers.
I'd get blown in alleys, suck the straights and queers.
I'd've fucked between trucks till the East turned red;
I'd embrace the millions just like Whitman said.

If I'd stayed in New York,
                                                I'd be dead.

# CHRISTOPHER LELAND

## After the Çemberlitaş Hamani

*for Constantine Cavafy*

And then you saw him.

Sweet irony, beside that pillar girdled, burnt,
the city's founding amulet, within its base
the sun rays of Apollo's crown, Palladium
of Troy, some shard of the True Cross,
the bloody nails of Jesus's Passion—
all immured there in your name.
You followed, swoony, as he led
down boulevards, then onto side streets,
into alleys—hopeless, radiant with hope—
through ghostly dusk until he ducks
into a doorway, there, beyond, some
hidden ruin—church or palace?—
overgrown and lush—or rank?—
with saplings, trees, with vines and
bush and flower. And then he turns, and,
fated, your lips taste that cat-like smile.

Thus was your beginning. He, no god,
just common clay, and yet, the mark made
without mercy by his knife upon your soul,
his fiery flesh alloyed with yours, the bed
he made for you that day upon the
leaves and earth and stones would be
yours ever after. Shamed of barren love,
still—long years later, back in Egypt—
you could not help but dream his
dream-like face, his purr as darkness
fell upon your frantic coupling.

His supple limbs, his chest, his pounding heart
and pounding blood still come to you
at night, emerging from the gloaming
which consumed him after he consumed you
left you there alone, forever changed.

# CHRISTOPHER LELAND

## The R&R/Michigan Avenue/Detroit

It's modesty, I guess.

No Boston attitude
nor New York guff,
Florida tan
or LA buff,
Bay excess
or Austin tough.

Opera fans and old-line rockers,
Connoisseurs and NASCAR clockers,
Chief execs and retail clerks,
Social workers, soda jerks,
Leather boys and orgy masters,
One-night-standers, deep romancers,
Art collectors, Vernor's drinkers,
Smart or dense, heroes and stinkers,
Bellied up at the R&R
downing beer from Mason jars.

Happy, chatty,
Black and white,
Love to dance,
Play pool.  No fights.
Old and young
from far and near.
Brother faggots.
Midwest queers.

## Douglas Dunes/The Woods/Night

Trees.

Like promises up-thrust
as blind men wander.
Bodies disembodied.
Floating free in to
and out of dark.

Demesne of touch:
a pinch, a pet, a kiss.

Without words.
This dark place
prefigures language.
Silent but for, far above,
the rub of branches.

Farther still, the throaty
hum of airplanes
plowing over this
calm earth of wants
resolved, unsaid.

Amidst the trunks, a pulse:
a solitary firefly.

And overhead, a shooting star
exploding green across the sky.

# WILLIAM REICHARD

## 35 South

Craning my neck to see the hawk
you just spotted on the telephone wire,
I see only low hills and fields.
After thirty years this land is invisible
to me, the route, pure habit.
I know things change.
The lanes shift, a house grows up
in the maple woods where, each spring,
green buckets are tied to the trunks
of the trees. My blindness is learned,
willful, even. If I don't see my world
slowly turning in on itself, then
that hawk will never catch the rabbit
that hides in the weeds.
I will never turn into the man
I don't want to become.

## Autumn Sequence

I.

In the unexpected heat of a late autumn day,
speak aloud all of those things you don't want.
Call them out by their names. They can't hide
in the sharp October light. They can't be buried
under brittle brown leaves. Say their names
and they'll appear, one by one. They'll look
at you. And then, they'll disappear.

II.

Everything smells so ripe and done.
Dry leaves skitter along the street.
Listless bees move from flower to flower
but nothing's left to eat.
My body wants to pull itself apart,
my limbs want to scatter themselves
among the weeds and wild asters.
Twenty years ago I didn't know
what a wild aster was, or why autumn
always brought me to my knees
in breathless fear and prayer.
Now I know why these things occur,
and I say, everything that has the will
to bloom is a flower.

III.

Wrens at the feeder in early November.
A single white cosmos blooms atop
a spindly stem. Blood red lily's stalks
are dry and brown, their leaves resemble
long blades. Some boys are going

# WILLIAM REICHARD

door to door, offering to rake or
bag leaves for cash. Everywhere,
houses in foreclosure. The inhabitants
abandon their lives. The neighborhood
fills with strays. A black cat approaches,
sweet and small. I give him some food
and water, and he quietly moves on.

## Sixteen


                    In slow circles,
across the ice,
we glide.
                    Midnight.

                    January.

                    Too drunk to care
about the open water
one hundred yards away.

                    This is what
we've come to call fun
in this quiet country.

                    In the back seat,
sandwiched between
Deb and Joy, best friends
since five, I sit.

                    Up front, driving,
sits the object
of my affection.

                    Confident, he
guides us across
the frozen lake.

                    The sky spins
wild with stars.

                    Powdery snow
engulfs the car
as it cuts through
virgin drifts.

# WILLIAM REICHARD

In my head,
an equilibrium, achieved with
cheap wine and desperation.

He, so quietly
aware of our mutual hunger,
is all I've ever wanted.

## Horses in Snow

Fading dusk turns the snow into stars,
the sky and the horizon line into
a black dome. The only world I know
exists in the twin beams of my headlights.
I'd forgotten what it's like, driving
a country road in a blizzard, the way
the wind swirls the snow across the road
in eddies, like water on a troubled lake.
I'd forgotten the hypnotic effect
of the flakes flying at the windshield,
how my eyes try to focus on each flake,
losing sight of the road itself.
I've never been afraid of night
in the city, but night in the country,
the storm enveloping everything,
makes all of the folk tales
true, all of the cautionary monsters
stalk the forest that fences in
the freeway. I am a child behind
the wheel, a boy sent on a man's errand
because there is no one else.
I drive slowly from village to village,
seeking out the safety that will not
be found. When the tires hit a patch
of ice, I'm pulled back into myself,
back into the doubled view of
the headlamps, and as the car reaches
the top of a rise, its lights shine
into a bend in the road, a pasture beyond.
There, for a moment, stand dozens
of horses. Some are still under
blankets of snow. Some are feeding
from hay-filled troughs. And one
is galloping, moving fast as me,
head down, trying to outrun the snow.

# JACK FRITSCHER

## Transistor Clock Radio (The Snows of 1969)

Long Michigander Days
I turn on the kitchen radio
to keep track of blizzard time
going into a room for no reason
going out of a room for no reason
I can't smelltouchtastefeel the audio.

"The official airport temperature
is one eight; that's eighteen degrees.
That's the 10:55 news, and now—
You know it!"
The tone hums.
It's the hour. 11 PM.
Silence (Can I hear it?)

The station jerks itself off crowing:
"CKLW Windsor!
THE BIG 8 JOCKS SOCKING IT TO YOU
24 HOURS A DAY; 50,000 WATTS BUT
SOUNDING LIKE A MILLION!
And now 4 in a row,
non-stop music from the station
that TURNS YOU ON!"

Somewhere out there
alone in his booth
the dickless-wonder jockey
gives the impression
of being a party,
stroking his antenna
with heavy beat,
sending his erect signal
out through the snow.

All that effort
when all I want
is to hear from him
the time
*what time is it*
trapping me snowbound
in the long rooms
of my silence
when all I want is
news snow plows
have cleared the lanes
of I-94 where men parked in rest stops
sit cruising in cars and trucks
tapping tail lights
in the red Morse code of sex.

# JACK FRITSCHER

## Clark Station: Kalamazoo 1969

Summer-parents, young, worn,
driving aimless past dusk
through the heat wave
circling through town
to cool off, cool down,
with wagon windows
overflowing with two wild tots,
green through the glass
in the buggy fluorescence
of this small filling station,
soft with light,
where I work late shifts alone,
inviting in the night
to a crowded husband
with a dollar bill
who stalls for time
for two and a half gallons
at 39.9 cents
to avoid going home
with his gum-popping bride
and his two squealing brats
pajama-ed for bed,
sweaty, sticky with candy,
whining for Coca-Cola.

In his rear-view mirror
he watches me,
hot, cool, twenty-six,
embarrassed for him
embarrassed for himself.
I crouch down to fill his tank.
Take your time, bud, he calls back,
elbow out his window,
biceps tattooed in Saigon,

winking in the side mirror,
nodding,
taking his moment with me.

Cap his tank
Take his dollar.
His fingers touch mine.
The bug zapper cracks purple lightning.
We laugh.
His eyes saving me up for later,
his grin, my grin, launching him,
So long, bud,
with his wife and fluorescent green kids
off into the darkness that is his alone,
with his hunting dog tied to a tree
out front of his house
with two cups
unwashed
in her kitchen sink.

# JACK FRITSCHER

## How Buddy Left Me

Some men can melt my heart
like Buck's boy Buddy from Butte,
wearing in the city
Montana boots and flannel shirts
smelling of soap and of himself:
curly, bearded, brooding,
all peace, love, and granola;
changing
to army surplus greens,
clipped to urban crewcut,
parted by pot away from me and Buck,
who wasn't much for touch anyway,
back in Butte,
where sons ride shotgun
in dad's pickup truck;
potted off in peace-less pieces,
granola gone, oh Buddy, on grass and acid,
and one night,
springing off the jump-seat of my Jeep,
snagging his green nylon Marine jumpsuit,
snagging what? Love?
With no end to the beginning
and no door slamming closed.
Somehow suddenly
we just let it go.

## Mapplethorpe

Caro Roberto! He loved cameras, Kools, Coke, and
for two years me flying round-trips together SFO JFK.
Lying in each other's post-coital arms slugabed on his mattress
on his black plank floor at 24 Bond Street,
his photographer's tongue licked my writer's eye,
in the morning rolling hard over me to reach the ringing phone,
saying "Ciao, Principessa," loving princesses and actresses
and dancers and the seven-foot calla lilies in my California garden.
"Patti's a genius," he confided, canonizing her face twinned with his,
screening me rushes of Patti in *Moving* and
*Robert Having His Nipple Pierced*
(with Patti keening poems on the soundtrack)
while his kitchen table caught fire from his forgotten cigarette.
There were always three people in his love affairs.
Gone, touring, singing, marrying someone else, widowed,
the Smith girl burned in his brain.
She was he and he was she in his solo portraits of her and himself.
At the after-hours Mineshaft bar, the democracy of anonymous sex
leveled the playing field of stardom, yet
he was a camera, cool, coked, aloof, a voyeur
turning the two floors of wild orgy into a casting call.
He ran his career like a department store,
ambushing trendy couples in SoHo galleries, saying,
"If you don't like this picture, you're not as avant garde as you think."
He was the goat-footed Pan, holding my hand in restaurants,
shopping together down Christopher Street for small Satanic bronzes
invoking Rimbaud and Verlaine, inspiring his own
famous flowers of evil, pistils and stamens, vaginas and cocks.
Late one night I sat in the gunsite of his camera
witnessing him work his process cool without drama.
I love you, he/I said, as he shot me.
At the end, dying young, he filmed flowers more than faces
because he could no longer stand eyes looking back at him
through the safety glass of his lens.
He loved. She loved. I loved.
I got his seed. Patti got his ashes.

# WALTER BECK

## Strange and Beautiful Skin

I came home
With my usual scent
Of cheap cigarettes and beer
Permeating my leather jacket.

On my flesh
Was the scent of new life
Blooming in the middle of nowhere;
The scent of coconut grease
And your strange flesh.

Pale skin
In the light of the cult film on TV
In your swank pad;
I'm not piss & vinegar
As much as the rest of the world thinks.

One night,
Two nights,
Or never again;
Just one moment
Of humanity
Without a fog of smoke and booze,
A soul unshackled
By the chains of an image.

Teach me
To love myself
And to love you;
Teach me
To be more than a glorified gofer,
A mercenary for hire
Who's feeling rapidly out-of-date and obsolete.

Teach me to be all the way alive.

## Plausible Deniability

Shots of me on stage
In rainbow suspenders
Rainbow stockings
With a rainbow wristband on;
It's still plausible deniability.

News footage rolling
Of me waving signs,
Proclaiming loudly & boldly
"EQUALITY OR DEATH";
It's still plausible deniability.

Pictures
Of me kissing an old camp buddy,
As an act of political protest;
A show of solidarity,
Making out on the streets of Indy;
It's still plausible deniability.

One staged photo
Of me grinning in the bright October sun,
The grin of the truly free,
With a sign in my hand
"BISEXUAL";
It's still plausible deniability.

My flag, my colors
Still strong from the streets
Hanging in a dirty wall tent,
Moldering away in the July heat;
It's still plausible deniability.

Until you see a photo
Of me screwing another guy
It's still plausible deniability.

# WALTER BECK

## Love is More than a Relationship

*for Kristian Holmes*

I sat in your cheap apartment;
Keeping your cat company
While you and your man
Shouted at each other on the other side.

You held me in my hotel room
And locked up the rest of my booze,
When I was too out of it
To care if I lived or died.

We kissed on a picket line,
In front of the cops and press.
One act of defiance,
There was no love behind it,
Only brotherhood and solidarity.

But it was our kisses
That would awaken the dogs and rats.

On the night I broke free,
When we kissed, both of us full of liberty and liquor;
One picture
Is worth 1,000 threats.

We could never be together;
We've been through too much together,
Seen too much,
Drank too much,
Lived too much.

To lay in physical embrace
Would cheapen everything.

## How to Measure a Man

You put the bike frame on the clamp,
The pedals screwed on first,
Then the training wheels,
If it's for a kid,
The front tire is next,
Then the handlebars,
Check the brakes and make sure everything is tight,
Add the bells and whistles.

Take it off the clamp,
Put it aside,
And put the next one up.

In the real world
That's all a man is worth.

# WALTER BECK

## Hoosier Swinging Both Ways Blues

It's a pretty boy's game here;
They want you to dance to Lady Gaga,
Instead of boogieing to John Lee Hooker.
They want you to quote *Glee*,
Instead of *Rocky Horror*.
They cover up their scars
With tans and make-up,
Instead of wearing them proudly
Like the badges of survival they should be.

They tell you
That you can't make up your own mind,
That you're just too afraid
To come all the way out.
They say you've never suffered for your love,
They tell you you're a just a coattail rider;
To them you're just greedy and confused.

When you're turned away
From a rally for your rights and dignity
By your own brothers and sisters
Just by the way you look,

They don't want no greasy freaks
Standing on their picket lines.
No long-haired weirdos
In ripped jeans and a tattered Judas Priest shirt
To stand beside them.

Their eyes give out one clear message:
"Not Welcome."

I don't let it get me down,
I don't let it break me;
As long as I have a song to sing,
I'm doing all right.

## I Can Still See You (A Life of Dreams)

I can still see you,
In your slinky evening gown
Strutting down the stage
Like the queen of all creation.

And I can still see you,
With my red fedora tipped to the crowd
To collect your tips.
And I remember
As you slipped a cigarette into my lip.

Yes, I can still see you too,
Your pale brown skin
Caressing me,
Tempting me.
Are my old roommates jealous
Of your fondness of me?

I can still see you,
Laughing at my Lenny Bruce records
In your dirty bohemian apartment.
Your work splashed across your walls,
Did you ever paint a picture of me?

I can still see all of you,
In the early morning hours
When the blues stretch out to the sunrise.

# JIM STEWART

## Picnic

The boy stood hidden in the stand
of silver poplars near the beach
and watched.

Men in faded Levis and white T-shirts
mowed the outfield near the pavilion.
Older boys, their shirts discarded,
wrestled sandbags in place for the bases.
Their young muscles strained and
sweat darkened new hair that peeked
from under arms.

A shirtless man he didn't know
helped one of the dads in a tight white wifebeater
install a new home plate in front of the rusted wire backstop.
The light breeze off Lake Michigan caressed
the curly hair on the stranger's chest.

The women called.
Potluck picnic was ready.
The boy flushed when others saw him step
from his hiding place.

When tables were cleared
and leftover casseroles
tucked in trunks for journeys home
no one saw he was not there
for hand-dipped ice cream cones.
No one heard the silence
when neither boys nor men
called out his name to join their teams.

The boy crouched behind
feral junipers near the lake where
crashing waves almost drowned
the cheers of men and boys at play.

AMONG THE LEAVES

## April Fools

It started as a dare

The very thought
of skinny dipping
in the lagoon
at Epworth Heights
excited them both
to a hard-on

The evening hike
down the beach
and over the dune
to the back of the links
gave them goose bumps

They quickly stripped
looking out at white caps
on the big lake
secretly pretending
not to notice
each other's erections

They jumped

The lagoon
so inviting in August
when they caddied
and inhaled each other's
summer sweat
will cool like
arctic springs in April

Boners gone
they dressed and sprinted
across the green
to the club for pizza

# JIM STEWART

## Eighteenth Summer

He cruised the John Deere
down long rows of tall trees
and picked up loaded pear crates
to deliver
at the fruit exchange

He swore it'd be his last summer on the farm
Fall would find him a freshman at State

He worked shirtless
to avoid a farmer's tan
that would belie his fantasy
of idle summer hours
on the nearby sandy beach

At day's end with migrant foreign voices gone
he seemed alone in the stillness of the dusk

Dismounted from the tractor
he took a leak and watched
the dusty path turn muddy
then saw a strong veined hand
offer a tawny ripened pear

He reached for the gift
from the young *bracero*
and savored the scent of
field sweat and fruit

A pair of orchard owls
called and answered
in the evening air

## Snow Fell

The new snowplow man
came yesterday
for the first time

He is young

His twenty-something
frame fills his faded Carhartts

He smiles a lot

Perhaps it's not to show
his perfect teeth
with Kodiak tobacco stains

There may be heavy snow
this year
enough to keep-at-bay
enlisting and
the war

# JIM STEWART

## At the Gas Station

One was a weekend dad
with no wedding band
but slightly surly sons
in his obligatory pickup truck

One was a stubble-faced farmer's son
home from college
for a family hunting weekend
with his brothers

Their eyes met
across the gas pumps
through
tangled rubber hoses

Each nodded

Indian Summer sweat
stained their well-worn
camouflage fatigues

Both topped off their tanks
and hankered for a drive to camp
where they could
hunt together

# Spring

Seed potatoes
onion sets
feeder pigs
farm signs

The farmer
shirtless in his
Oshkosh bibs
attends his roadside stand

Mid-day sweat
beads lightly on his ivory skin
dampening blond Viking hair
that peeks shyly from beneath
his strong young arms

You watched
as he rubber-banded bundles
of purple-headed asparagus sprouts
then slowly cleaned
his thick thumbs

You forgot his name
until by the courthouse
you saw it
on a fallen-heroes plaque

# WHITTIER STRONG

## Seventeen Below

I never noticed my nose hairs
until my first Minnesota winter. When I set foot
in the chill, each follicle stood
at attention, a platoon
protecting my precious lungs
to no avail. A blazing cold
marched through my trachea, bronchi, alveoli.
My fingers,
believing they were on a suicide mission,
attempted in vain to leap off my hands.
My quadriceps, naked
as a stranded soldier through my fashionably thin
jeans, felt massive and immobile, tanks
out of gas. Only my feet,
bunkered inside my boots, withstood
the onslaught unfazed.

I learnt the next year
how to boost the troops' morale:
armor my face with a muffler wrapped round,
fortify my fingers with doubled-up stretch gloves,
fuel my legs with long johns.
The boots could weather
the battle on their own.

## Minnesota/Indiana

People ask me why I moved to Minnesota, sight unseen, knowing no one,
from the great state of Indiana, where I and ten generations past had
  been born.
I tell them that the Scandinavian Land of Ten Thousand Lakes
is in every way opposite the Scots-Irish Crossroads of America.

I tell them that a Twin Cities recession
looks like the most robust economy my hometown has ever known,
and I speak of the ease here with which I get from point A to point B,
and that back home, "rush hour" means two busses an hour (give or take).
Here I am loud and proud, a rainbow arcing through the city,
but there, the slightest sashay invites epithets—faggot, queer.
Here, when things got lowest, I fell into the safety net,
but there, when I hit bottom, they simply snipped the strings.
I tell them that I'll take roads that are always being worked on
over roads that are never being worked on,
and that three months of nine-below-zero in comfortable layers
are better by far than three months of ninety degrees in uncomfortable
  anything.

Even though "Minnesota Nice" means thinking twice about what anyone
  says,
and back home, "Say what you mean, mean what you say" is the order of
  the day,
though I have to doctor the water with lemon and lime and Crystal
  Light
instead of refreshing body and soul straight from the tap,
even if here, when I take a walk, I worry about muggings and flash gangs
and there, an evening stroll merely means negotiating the sidewalkless
  streets . . .

I'll take the place that has always said to me, "Welcome"
over the place that has always told me, "Go away."

# WHITTIER STRONG

## *Pas de deux*

Why would I not have thought
we would dance forever? Are not the dancers to mirror
each other in the dance?  I stepped to my left, he
glided to his right. I leant, he
caught me—breathless—my
partner at last.

We could have swirled, slid, sashayed into a seductive
tango, but I never learnt to lead. Instead, we fell into a stately
minuet. When the violinists laid
down their bows, so did Cupid. And he, partner
no more, bowed and bid adieu, I
solo once more.

## My Grandma's Print of Gainsborough's *Blue Boy*, 1987

A full score and ten years have I stood vigil
Upon the wall of this stale drawing-room,
Always to gaze through the smoke-blue haze
At the bookcase accumulating yearly
Such a gauche, dismal array of curios,
It has become a Louvre of poor taste.

A full score and ten years have I witnessed
Four generations of this fecund clan
Plod through and flop down upon
This shabby trash they dare call furniture
To weave the rope of bitterness, malice, and gossip
That binds this piteous family together.

A full score and ten years have I borne
The filth of smoke and sickly stench of age
Upon my delicate silks and azure velvets
Rendered in oil and fused to paperboard,
Imprisoned for aye within a frame of wood
And knowing that I am born to far better.

# WHITTIER STRONG

## Tanica Saunders

**Experience**
tells us that a name is a name, no matter the diktats of the
"name Nazis" and the baby-name books. Parents cannot predicate
the path of their offspring through the choice of a name.
Try telling that to some people.
Take the case of Tanica Saunders:
Accounting B.A.,
three-point-eight GPA, while
raising a baby.
Honor society,
student government,
prestigious internship. All the

**Qualifications**
an employer would want. Yet the hiring manager
has rejected her résumé in record time. The name, you see. It's
ghetto, gutter, utterly
inappropriate for their world-class firm.
Never mind the meaning. Named for Aunt
Tanya, who died in a drive-by at twenty-five. Named for Grandma
Monica, who took in Mama
when her boyfriend abandoned her. None of this

**Interests**
Hiring Manager Jennifer. She has already constructed
Tanica's life story: a girl from the 'hood,
who wears hoodies to work,
a new baby every year and a new boyfriend every two, certainly
dealing on the side. This would surprise
Tanica's suburban neighbors and husband, for sure. But
Jennifer has already moved on to the next résumé,
a superb young candidate named
Amy, a functional alcoholic who
cheated to a three-point-three. Yes,
she will do nicely.

## The Cabin

Built to withstand the most brutal
Minnesota winter, it still should have crumbled
in a heap by now. The years
still showed, the steps corroded long ago,
the windows but shards, paint
yielded to mold. Odor of mildew hung as a shroud
in the guts of the cabin. Blown-about leaves sheltered
mouse nests in corners. Musty
flannel blankets lay about in random
heaps. Piles of crumpled beer cans and faded
pornography and forgotten weed
were strewn across the deteriorating
avocado-green rug.

Katie, likewise crumpled and strewn,
lay beneath one of the blankets. Her limp, long, dirty-blond
hair had not been washed in a week. She opened sad
gray raccoon eyes and rolled out from under the blanket. Thin
green sweater, tight blue jeans: all that defied
the April morning chill. She stood—an awkward fawn—
and stretched her spindly arms. To the door,
then, one foot in front of the other along the planks
that served as a makeshift entry. To survive
meant never returning "home"—what home?—
it was never home. Onward,
ever onward, that was the only way.

# GREGG SHAPIRO

## Extraordinary Measures

What's the difference between running
in place or in circles? You still get there
at the same time. Too late, out of breath,
empty-handed. I still call out the names

of the dead. Awake, asleep, mid-air.
Moving my lips with or without my voice,
waving my hands to no avail. This is
the age of responsibility. Every breath

an accusation, a finger stabbing the air.
Whispers, murmurs of education and
prevention. Advice given from behind
a hand. Ask yourself what you would

do, what distance you would travel to
save a friend, a family member, a stranger.
No length too great, no act too ordinary.
I pinch myself awake from the same

drowning dream. Starless, airless, endless.
Water black as rock, warm as a motor.
Swimming is out of the question, arms
heavy as corpses. The drowned float

past, under the surface. Bottleless messages
to the living on the shore. Give rage
a face, a mouth twisted into goodbye.
Two moist eyes that see everything

unblinking. A nose for trouble and ears
to listen for the sound of nurses shuffling
silently on schedule to monitor a fever,
a pulse, to preserve and protect what is left.

## Winter Work

What a body knows about temperature. Varying degrees.
The boiling point and ice. Throaty hum of snow-blowers,
the metallic scrape of trucks and plows. You could learn

something from this; endurance, appreciation for seasons,
anticipation. Always watching the sky, changing cloud

formations for signs, indications of spring's approach.
Until the difference is apparent, certain precautions must
be taken. Fur and insulating feathers. Chains on tires.

Salt-stained leather, rosy cheeks. Grow accustomed to
the costumes. Nothing changes winter's mind. Dream

of escaping to a tropical climate. You wonder how you
got here in the first place. Confuse reason with excuses.
Throw another log, old newspapers, your passport on the fire.

# GREGG SHAPIRO

## Domestic Disturbance

Is it possible to feel affection for a bed?
After almost 20 years of gay wedded bliss and
a vast assortment of mattresses—full, pillow-top
queen and standard queen—a super-firm king-size
mattress has brought renewed tranquility to our home
and rest. There is room enough for the pack *to sleep,*
*perchance to dream*, without disturbing one another.
Fidgety and golden Dusty still prefers the floor rug,

where she can mutter and run in her sleep without
waking us. But when she finds the strength to lift
her less limber 11-year-old body onto the bed, she
is aware that there is a place for her. Red and white
k.d. has a newfound respect for her spot at the foot
of the big bed where she no longer has to dodge
Rick's restless legs or my alternately hot and cold
feet, seeking and shunning cover without warning.

Does a dog's bowel or bladder troubles belong
in a poem? In our post-sleep study slumber, Rick's
breathing apparatus provides him with sound sleep
while filling the bedroom with the resonance of silent
snoring and measured white noise. If Rick could
sleep through virtually anything before, including
his own lack of breath intake and release, then
nothing short of a massive earthquake or his alarm

clock can wake him now. So, it falls to me when
Dusty or k.d. experiences any kind of bodily function
anguish, in the hours between when we lay our heads
on our plumped and respective pillows and when we
awake. It's not unusual to go outside in flannel pajama
bottoms or track pants and a sweatshirt, flip-flops or
Adidas shower slides, speedily walking one or both
of the dogs down the sidewalk or in the passageway

between the buildings heading east or west toward
or away from one of the parks in all kinds of weather
in the pre-dawn hours, with one or two full and knotted
poop  bags in hand. Tonight the alley between our street
and Argyle is free of the raccoon duo who once appeared
out of thin air at two a.m. to remind us that, at that appointed
hour, the turf and the night belonged to them. We hurried
inside when we saw them, slammed the door and latched

the bolt, listening from the safety of the garage to hear
if they would come sniffing or scratching, or if they were
satisfied just to see us startled and running away. Perhaps
they kept their distance because of the blood-rattling shouts
and screams emanating from the half-open window of
the multi-unit dwelling across the alley. Fury-fueled
accusations and declarations, threats of violence and
bodily injury. Witnessed from a distance, it colors

the night darker, whips the air like frost. Back in bed,
I dream of stray bullets piercing brick and mortar, wood
and sheetrock, finding their way to my spine or chest,
Rick's skull or thigh. Clouds in the shape of numbers
—911—hover just out of reach. Blankets transform into
camouflage Kevlar vests. The dogs sleep unaware.

# GREGG SHAPIRO

## Talking Back to a Knife

"Hello. You've reached the Miller residence—but no one lives here anymore."
— A telephone-answering message recorded by Ann M. Miller before she killed
herself, her two children, three dogs and parakeet last week. (*Newsweek* 9/27/93)


The other night I dreamed she was my mother. Distraught
after another of my father's business schemes went belly-up.
Defeated after repeated attempts to get him to quit smoking,

eat better and exercise more. Maybe it was just all the years
of listening to him snore, chew with his mouth open. We are
there, still her children in our grown-up bodies, obedient to
a fault. She herds us downstairs into the basement. On our
knees, we brush away cobwebs at the entrance to the crawlspace.

She seals windows with roll after roll of electrical tape, dusty
remainders from my father's cracked leather sample-case from
when he was a fixative and adhesive salesman. Her cheeks

puff out like a cartoon fish as she extinguishes the pilot light
with one breath. In the dark, she is the barrel of a gun,
illuminated by the gunpowder blast, baptism of bullets.
She is a blade, her distorted reflection like a sideshow mirror.
She is reminded, even in exaggeration, of how pretty she is.

How much we, her children, look like her. She thinks she
could eat the knife, she is that hungry. She knows there are
animals who eat their young and her appetite flashes like

the sweat on Medea's brow. Or maybe it was Naamah,
Noah's wife, children and animals in close quarters, on
a journey to who knows where, while her life rained down
around her. Maybe, I think. Might. If only. I wonder
with which one of these mythic women Ann M. Miller

identified. How old was she? How old were her children?
How many dog years to add to the equation? When did she
stop finding humor in little things? A flat tire in a shopping

mall parking lot or a late child-support check. I imagine her
in her fragrant kitchen, the blue-breasted parakeet chipping
away at a birdseed bell in a cage across the room. Two dogs
napping under a window, bathed in a patch of autumn sunlight.
The third dog's tags clanking against her water bowl, as she

drinks it dry. The children in another room, playing a video
game about hidden treasure, warlocks, winged horses. Ann
selects the sharpest knife she can find and dices an onion

for her children's dinner. The sound, as the blade pierces
the skin, a cross between cough and cackle, a voice she has
learned to ignore, to suppress like a sneeze. "Don't look
now," it says, "the walls are crumbling." "As if I need you
to remind me," Ann says, the onion bringing buried tears

to the surface, which she wipes away with the back of her
hand. "You don't need to stick me more than once to know
that I'll cry out or cut me very deeply to know that I'll bleed."

# CHRISTOPHER HENNESSY

## Dreaming Through the Fifth Day Without Power

*The Great Ice Storm of 1976, Mid-Michigan*

Tarpaulin tent-flap winks opens on-
to the sweating wall of fire, a new in-
side. Outside, latticed with spun-
sugar, our birchwoods. All skin-
close, mom and dad shiver-
pink all night, my dreams still-
born in fever-sleep and yet . . .

      \*

I walk naked through a dying
orchard. Smolder-fat apples
of charcoal fall to the ground,
winter seeds that crackle, dim
and begin their dream to earth's core,
to perfect-memory: *touch me*
—& a heat like the white-eyes of ice.

## Dream the Bull

### I.

She told you about me, your mother did.
I was her nightmare in the years of the black
bread, the mud gods, the fist-cut-off.

She told you, your mother, I chased her,
my fur a black igneous rock, the vermillion
snarl of my tongue, my shoulder bashing open

the gate, where motherhood was kept down—
where there is no peck, no claw, no carving,
knives sawing through the buck of chicken bones.

There is only blood,
or only there is no blood
but for the want of it.

### II.

She did not say, your mother, I was only bull
in name. She didn't want you knowing only a man
can woo me back into the body of a boy.

Only a man knows how to fool me, a slash
of his piss in the snow, a liquid cut to take me
off her scent. Why am I telling you this, you

fearful of a rooster's hiss, so sure the dark
cavern of the grain silos hold monsters even I
dream of? Because you are in her dream, too, boy-

not-yet-born. As I stomp in the shit, my black hide
as shining as the devil's sooty kiss, you are on my back,
spiteful thighs gripping my flanks like a lover.

# CHRISTOPHER HENNESSY

## Sleeping Bear Dunes

A hard pouring over Lake Michigan flecks a constellation of wet
sequins onto the backs of a great brown bear and her two cubs as
they paddle through the rough waves to escape the roar of a burning
woods that was home, as they swim for a shore they can't see,
mother leading her babies
                    to what will become a brutal but
beautiful dune on Lake Michigan, where a little boy will one day cry
into his father's arms, and his wails will send the gulls, warblers, and
mergansers fleeing into the mirror blue of the sky,
                                where they will
seek out the Great Spirit Manitou to tell him of the child's pain and
bring him (sly birds!) beakfuls of sweet bearberries, a gift to favor
the child
                whose young father has tried to teach the boy how to
know the trees—juniper and jack pine, beech and maple, hemlock,
basswood, and black cherry—that line the route to the dunes, mark
the way to its peaks, where, finally,
                         high above the water on a dune
the shape of a back arched in pain, the young father tells the old
Ojibwe story of how two cubs were too weak for the Lake's roil, of
how the fire on the far share burned so bright it lit their drowning
for the mother bear, as she watched from the eastern shore.
                                     As he
speaks, the father skips flat, round stones into the Great Lake, and
his expert wrist flick (practiced for years with his own old man)
make the stones sing out over the white tufts of surf, a *clap—clap-
clap—clap* of two huge invisible hands, but the boy is still crying,
not because his father's story is a sad one, not because he is a simple,
sensitive boy who sometimes sucks his thumb . . . though all of that
is true, but because
                    he can see—can really see!—the bears as they
paw through the waves, tiring from the pound and bone-soak of
the lake's pull, can see the cubs slip beneath the icy lake, can feel the
mother bear's iridescent black eyes on him, hears her breath, still
coming heavy after the long swim, her back hunched in exhaustion
but her head raised, her nose sniffing the freshwater air for her cub's

                                      

scent. "She will always be like this,"

the father tries to comfort;
"the Ojibwe's Great Spirit sees the mother's love, pities her grief
and raises her cubs from the lake's deep well of souls. The Spirit
transforms them into the tiny Manitou islands—see, we can see
them from here—and now the mother bear, still at watch, rests here,
the slope of these dunes her body."

All of this, and the boy
cannot be comforted by the end of the story, by the father's hands
smoothing his hair, lifting him high on his shoulders so he can see
the blue belly of the lake, the relentless watery horizon, no shore in
sight, because the promise his father gives is an unreachable island, a
buried sleep, a singing stone that sinks

as soon as it's out of sight.

# CHRISTOPHER HENNESSY

## First Sunday

Slim black Bibles, red
hymnals, a moon-
faced man, starched

spine, robed in white.
Me: a package tied tight
in a tiny brown suit.

Rays of winter sun beat
through glass pictures, burn
-ish my face in ruby, orange.

In songs the church is a lung,
the organ wheezes, and I hear
the bleat of lamb, a whimper.

Is that me, my little cry? Is my
bow-tied gut worming its way
out of my body? My buttoned

chest swells as if it might
pop open and release
a bearded old man, shaking

his god-sized fists at me.
My own tiny hands drop
my Bible—its hot, black skin

the scale of a snake, coiled,
waiting to strike. A single urge
surges from gut to throat:

to stomp the snake
back to the black ink
of its—and all—origin.

## Strawberries

I tiptoe through their leaf-tucked beds,
secretly hoping to feel a glandular wriggling—

my fat fingers scrabble through the patch,
too timid to pull at the feverish bulbs of red heart,

throbbing and slick with dew. Pimpled.
Gorged. Unwell. Gorgeous.

But oh, I love the taste of the unripe, pubescent,
to feel the pebbled bitter in my mouth.

Gathering in the scoop of my t-shirt as I squat
among them, I take only the pinkest stones.

# RAYMOND LUCZAK

## Bile

1.

Growing up, I loved nothing more
than candies and ice cream.
I rarely gained a pound.
I was a swizzle stick.

2.

The first twangs of pain crept at first.
Suddenly its talons dug deep
into the underside of my ribcage.
Mortality had finally paid a visit.

3.

Out on the schoolyard I was an effigy.
Calling me names just out of earshot
was the intonation of my daily funeral mass.
I died but my hearing aids didn't.

4.

It's official: my gallstones should be removed.
The function of bile, my surgeon says,
is to help break down the fats in my stomach.
My gallbladder is the reservoir of bile.

5.

I once wanted nothing but cures for my acne.
My face was a globe pockmarked with volcanoes

that would erupt pus once I sterilized my fingers.
Sometimes if they didn't explode, I cried lava.


6.


My surgeon says she will make four incisions:
one in my belly button, one between my front ribcage,
and two directly over my gallbladder.
A tiny camera will slither inside, its sole eye beaming.


7.


Learning the language of hands was key
to my recovery. I no longer sickened from their looks.
Knowing that my hands could soufflé words
in ways they couldn't was a just dessert.


8.


Doctor, do not take out my gallbladder. I'm not ready.
I need more bile. I've been far too sweet
for too long. Please do not take away
all my pain. I've yet to master the recipe of rage.

# RAYMOND LUCZAK

## The Birch Tree

A lifetime ago when I'd never thought
in terms of decades passing,
my father planted a small birch sapling
on the west border between our house
and the house we rented out next door.

Growing up, it's seen us nine children
chase the winds in the backyard and move away.
Each time we visit, we're always surprised
by how tall, even angrily, it overlooks
my mother's creaky swinging bench.

A makeshift shack, made of discarded lumber
and siding, used to sit right there,
but it was torn down after one summer.
The other shack was enough.
That too was eventually torn down.

It has also seen our family dog die
of a heat stroke in the sun.
Then the vegetable gardens were carpeted
with grass. The dirt basketball court
disappeared with the dog house too.

The gnarly apple tree that lent shade
to our lanky picnic table was cut down.
The clothesline stretched between the two T's
is the only thing left. Even now it's hanging
onto freshly washed clothes waving bye-bye.

After so many summers of betrayal
and abandonment, it knows that one day
it will get chopped down like so many others.
But not now. Oh, not now, not ever,
not while I still have a lifetime left to go.

## Lakewood Cemetery

*for S. W. G.*

The man I could've been had you loved me
lies buried mute, unmarked among tombstones.

His eyes once lit up like daffodils,
startling whispers of the spring to come.

I have flowers but no vase to place them
next to this freshly potted rectangle.

My body, not quite emptied of you, roots
in embraces gnarly and brittle as bones.

Soil sludges through my veins until I worm
close to the ghost reduced to nights alone.

I tell him that he was not wrong to love you.
He grunts, turns over, and goes back to sleep.

The atlas of your uncashed affections
creeps wrinkly rivers all over his back.

Flickers of regret tickle his eyelids.
A stranded cicada scuttles away.

# RAYMOND LUCZAK

## On the Corner of Oak and Spruce

*for D. C.*

On the corner of Oak and Spruce
once stood a magnificent oak tree.
Come autumn it was not shy with its acorns
that then took refuge, furrowing deep
like stones among the grass blades.

Many summers ago I ran barefoot.
The cool green carpet soothed me like lotion
after each tiptoe across a stripe
of baked tar, a band-aid
just melted in a crumbly fissure.

The oak tree has been chopped down
a long time ago. Potholes have proliferated
worse than acorns. Even Norrie School's closed.
There are more FOR SALE signs than neighbors.
My mother has problems with her hip.

The patches across the street where I'd plucked
strawberries have vanished. The prickly roses too.
The thick trees near the cracked cement floor
have given way to a cavalcade of birch in the distance.
It's not the country of my childhood.

Not as many streetlights there stay awake as I do,
and when I do, I catch the silhouette of you
standing tall in the canopy of constellations.
You are an oak tree. I await the fall of your acorns
into my arms, soil enriched with memory.

## The Gynoecium

*from Ancient Greek:* gene, *meaning* woman, *and* oikos; house

Aphrodite and Venus thus wedded:
Let us be less afraid of each other,
these strangely familiar curves
of our long-hidden bodies,
victim of too many doubt-filled winters
in the faces of men crawling everywhere,
these unfamiliar folds opening
like rose petals revealing pistils tipped
with passion-fruit nectar. Each sip
we tender each other is a dew drop
each morning after a night's rain
deep in the peat of our pillows,
entangling the waxy hair of dreams
among the squirming of worms.
Let us breathe dawn's heady oxygen,
circulate water in our veins,
and cling: such sweet caffeine!
Each day we will photosynthesize
the sun's brutal stares into softness,
the full greenery of mothering
the baby poems nestling among
our feet never leaving
but always wriggling toes,
itching for another kiss, another sigh.
Let us move together as one,
two flowers entwined in embrace
against the winds, awaiting
the blessing of bees spreading
the bloom of our new address.

# MICHAEL KIESOW MOORE

## The "Betty" Morris Dancer

In groups of six, the Morris dancers gamble
on the newly green hill. Dressed in white, the
men cavort in their timeless choreography.

White handkerchiefs fly like spritely doves,
bells strapped to their ankles jangle the cadence
of first spring—leaping, manly arabesques.

Watchers of the festivity spy a little girl,
wearing a dress the color of hummingbird red,
twirling a bright red parasol, daintily.

"How pretty you are," says a stranger.
"Thank you, I'm dressed just like my grandpa."
"Honey, you mean your grandmother."

"Nope. My dress is just like my grandpa's."
"No. You mean your grandmother's."
A burly man galumphs to the girl's side,

all white beard and hairy legs.
He wears a dress the color of hummingbird red,
twirling a bright red parasol, daintily.

## Girls

It isn't just the fey boys who die.
Girls are killing themselves, too.
Girls who rather wear baggy jeans and dad's Marine Corps sweatshirts
    than pink skirts and yellow sweaters.
Girls who like to toss a football.
Girls who are not skinny as Barbie.
Girls who would not be caught dead wearing lipstick.
Girls forbidden to enter the locker-room, taunted with the words, "You're
    a guy!"
Girls who forget their own names because every day they are called
    Dyke, Queer, Faggot, Freak, Transvestite, Butch, Cunt, Slut, Skank,
    Prostitute, Hooker, Whore.
Girls who look tough on the outside.
Girls who cry in hidden places.
Girls who cannot take it any more.

# MICHAEL KIESOW MOORE

## The Visitor

I lay in bed, trying to sleep,
trying to forget one more terrible
day in elementary school.
I hated recess more than anything else,
even more than gym class.
The worst things mostly did not
happen in gym.
Recess was different.
They could get away with anything there.
I asked my teachers to let me stay indoors.
They always set me out.

That day I peered carefully at the playground lot.
I didn't see them. Was I free?
I ran out, feeling light.
The sun felt warm on my skin.
I could breathe.
Suddenly I was face down on the asphalt.
One of them had tripped me.
They surrounded me, hitting me,
calling me Fatso, Sissy, Crybaby.
All the other children surrounded us,
watching my humiliation.
After a while a teacher broke through,
made the beating stop. As he led me
to the nurse's office, the only words he
said to me was: "You should learn to
fight back."

As I lay in bed, eyes wide open,
praying never to go
back to school again, I became aware
of a presence, a man sitting at the
end of the bed. He was fairly lean,
not fat like me, and he looked at
me with a kind look, so different

from how most adults frowned
at me. "Just survive," he said.
"I am your older self. I am here
to tell you that you will get to the
other side of these terrible times."

I blinked. He looked so real,
so solid. Comfortable in his body.
Could I really grow up to be him?
"This is the worst. Right now.
Just survive. You'll be glad you did."

Sometimes when I am in bed,
trying to fall asleep, I send thoughts
to my boy self, telling him
to survive. That this is the worst.
There will be reason to endure,
that there is another side.
I hope my younger
self gets the message.
I hope that he lives.

# MICHAEL KIESOW MOORE

## Gay Straight Alliance

They gather together,
the teenagers who survive.
They remember,
they cry,
they hold on,
hold each other.

How you label
yourself does not matter.
You are welcome.
Here, in this space,
you are *safe*.

There is only one rule:
be yourself.
In this space,
you *will* be accepted.
That's another rule.

They are finding
each other.

Across the land.
They are coming home.

## What to Pray For

I once met one of the angels who scribe our prayers. The angel appeared as you would expect: beautiful and fearsome. "Do you get tired of transcribing our prayers?" I asked it. The angel sighed and the earth shook with the sound. "Give me this, give me that. Help me find love. Make me skinny. Make me young. I could go on." Then I asked, "Are all prayers written down?" The earth shook again. "All prayers are heard." I pitied the angel, a strange feeling. "What prayers *should* we make?" I asked. The angel gave answer:

"Give thanks for all the ways you are *not* angels. That your lives are so brief, that change is your only constant, that you know what despair is, that you are a work in a progress that will never finish. Ask for new questions with each answer. Ask that you become comfortable with uncertainty. Ask for our help to remove your fears so that fearlessly you stoke the love you carry inside and reveal yourself as a pillar of light only you can attain. Pray that you learn how to blind angels with your light."

# CONTRIBUTORS

**WALTER BECK**'s poems have been published in the *ISU Tonic, VU Tecumseh Review, The Q Review, Off the Rocks, Burner, subTerreanean,* and others. He is the Poet Laureate of Camp Krietenstein. His first two chapbooks *Life Through Broken Pens* and *Some Assembly Required* were published by Writing Knights Press this year. Beck grew up in the suburbs of Indianapolis, and lives in Avon, IN. [passedoutfullyclothed.blogspot.com]

**AHIMSA TIMOTEO BODHRÁN** is the author of *Antes y después del Bronx: Lenapehoking* (New American Press) and the editor of an international queer Indigenous issue of *Yellow Medicine Review: A Journal of Indigenous Literature, Art, and Thought.* An American Studies Ph.D. candidate at Michigan State University, he is completing *Yerbabuena/Mala yerba, All My Roots Need Rain: mixed-blood poetry & prose.* [msu.edu/~bodhran]

**JAMES CIHLAR** is the author of the poetry books *Rancho Nostalgia* (Dream Horse Press, 2013), *Undoing* (Little Pear Press, 2008), and *Metaphysical Bailout* (Pudding House Press, 2010). His writing appears in *American Poetry Review, Prairie Schooner, Lambda Literary Review, Smartish Pace, Court Green, Mary,* and *Forklift, Ohio.* He teaches literature at the University of Minnesota and creative writing at Macalester College. [twitter.com/jamescihlar]

**JACK FRITSCHER**, born 1939, Illinois; Loyola University, Chicago, Ph.D. dissertation: Tennessee Williams (1967); first poem published (1957); 55-year professional writing career: 20 books, hundreds of gay press short stories, features, photos; founding San Francisco editor of legendary *Drummer* magazine; Robert Mapplethorpe's lover/biographer; historian writing books *Gay San Francisco* and Lammy Finalist *Some Dance to Remember*; writer-director of 150 safe-sex erotic features, Palm Drive Video. [jackfritscher.com]

**BRENT GOODMAN** is the author of *Far From Sudden* (2012) and *The Brother Swimming Beneath Me* (2009) as well as the chapbooks *Wrong Horoscope* (1999) and *Trees are the Slowest Rivers* (1998). His poems have appeared in *Poetry, Pleiades, The Beloit Poetry Journal, Gulf Coast, Cimarron Review, Zone 3,* and elsewhere. He lives and works in Rhinelander, WI. [brentgoodman.info]

**GEORGE KLAWITTER** taught literature at St. Edward's University in Austin until his retirement back to Indiana in 2012. His poems have been printed in various journals including *The James White Review, Poetry Northwest, Poet Lore, Borderlands,* and *Evergreen Chronicles.* His first book of poetry, *Country Matters,* appeared in 2001, and his book *Let Orpheus Take Your Hand* won the Gival Press Poetry Prize in 2002.

**CHRISTOPHER LELAND** is an American writer and educator. He is the author of five novels, a literary history of Argentine fiction of the 1920s, and two books on the craft of writing as well as various poems and translations from the Spanish. His most recent title is the story collection *Love/Imperfect* (Wayne State University Press, 2011). He lives in Detroit and teaches at Wayne State University.

**RAYMOND LUCZAK** has written and edited 15 books, including *Men with Their Hands: A Novel* (Queer Mojo, 2009) and *Eyes of Desire 2: A Deaf GLBT Reader* (Handtype Press, 2007). His five poetry collections include *How to Kill Poetry* (Sibling Rivalry Press, 2013) and *Mute* (A Midsummer Night's Press, 2010). He is the editor of *Jonathan*. A native of Michigan's Upper Peninsula, he lives in Minneapolis. [raymondluczak.com]

**JOHN MEDEIROS** is a poet and memoirist whose work has appeared in numerous literary journals. He is the author of *couplets for a shrinking world* and is the recipient of numerous awards for his writing, including *Gulf Coast*'s nonfiction award and two Minnesota State Arts Board grants. An excerpt from his forthcoming memoir, *Self, Divided*, has been named a Notable Essay in *Best American Essays 2006*. [jmedeiros.net]

**STEPHEN S. MILLS** grew up in Richmond, Indiana. He holds an M.F.A. from Florida State University. His poems have appeared in *PANK*, *The New York Quarterly*, *The Antioch Review*, *The Los Angeles Review*, *Knockout*, *Assaracus*, and others. His first book, *He Do the Gay Man in Different Voices*, is out from Sibling Rivalry Press. [stephensmills.com]

**MICHAEL KIESOW MOORE** is a published and award-winning writer whose work has appeared in periodicals including *Talking Stick*, *Water~Stone Review*, *Evergreen Chronicles*, *The James White Review*, and the book *Losing Loved Ones to AIDS*. Michael has received a Minnesota State Arts Board fellowship, and he teaches creative writing at the Loft Literary Center. Michael curates the Birchbark Books Reading Series. [michaelkiesowmoore.com]

**TIMOTHY MURPHY**, a Dakota poet, published his most recent three books last year with the Fort Mandan Foundation, with three more titles coming out in 2013. A fuller biography can be found on Wikipedia under Timothy Murphy, poet. [fortmandan.org]

**WILLIAM REICHARD** is a writer, editor, and educator with four published collections of poetry, most recently *Sin Eater* (2010) and *This Brightness* (2007), both from Mid-List Press. He is the editor of the anthology *American Tensions: Literature of Identity and the Search for Social Justice* (New Village Press, 2011). Reichard grew up in Smith's Mill, MN and currently lives in Saint Paul, MN. [williamreichard.com]

**JAMES SCHWARTZ** was born on February 19, 1978 and raised in the Old Order Amish community. He currently lives in Three Rivers, MI. He is the author of *The Literary Party: Growing Up Gay and Amish in America* (inGroup Press, 2011). [literaryparty.blogspot.com]

**GREGG SHAPIRO** is the author of the chapbook *GREGG SHAPIRO: 77* (Souvenir Spoon Press, 2012) and the poetry collection *Protection* (Gival Press, 2008). Shapiro is also a Chicago-based entertainment journalist whose interviews and reviews run in a variety of regional LGBT publications and web sites.

# CONTRIBUTORS

**JIM STEWART** grew up on a farm in Michigan. After 20 years he retired from the Chicago Public Library, moved to a 19th-century farmhouse by Lake Michigan, and started to write. His first book, *Folsom Street Blues: A Memoir of 1970s SoMa and Leatherfolk in Gay San Francisco*, won several awards including a Gold e-Lit for Erotic Non-Fiction. His poetry has appeared in various publications.

**WHITTIER STRONG** is a true Midwestern boy, having spent virtually his entire life in Indiana, Missouri, and Minnesota. He is a Creative Writing undergraduate at Metropolitan State University, where he is on the editorial staff of the school's arts and literary magazine, *Haute Dish*. He performs as a part of the Twin Cities Gay Men's Chorus. He resides in Minneapolis. [whittierstrong.wordpress.com]

**MALCOLM STUHLMILLER** grew up in North Dakota, graduated with a B.A. in English literature from the University of Minnesota in Minneapolis, and lives in Minneapolis and on the North Shore of Lake Superior with his partner of 30 years and their two cats. Writing short poems is a perfect pastime for his Myers Briggs ENFP profile. He loves doing the laundry and wearing nice hats.

**SCOTT WIGGERMAN**, author of *Presence* and *Vegetables and Other Relationships*, grew up in the Chicago suburb of McHenry before heading in his 20s to Austin, Texas, where he and his partner co-founded Dos Gatos Press, publisher of the annual *Texas Poetry Calendar* and books like *Wingbeats: Exercises and Practice in Poetry*. Like Scott and his partner, the *TPC* is in its fifteenth year. [swig.tripod.com]

www.ingramcontent.com/pod-product-compliance
Lightning Source LLC
LaVergne TN
LVHW011244080426
835509LV00005B/629